UNDERSTANDING THE BRITISH IRON AGE: AN AGENDA FOR ACTION

A Report for the Iron Age Research Seminar
and
the Council of the Prehistoric Society

by

C. Haselgrove, I. Armit, T. Champion, J. Creighton, A. Gwilt,
J.D. Hill, F. Hunter, and A. Woodward

September 2001

Published 2001 by the Trust for Wessex Archaeology Ltd
Portway House, Old Sarum Park, Salisbury SP4 6EB
Wessex Archaeology is a Registered Charity No. 287786

on behalf of the Iron Age Research Seminar and the Prehistoric Society

British Library Cataloguing in Publication Data
A catalogue entry for this book is available from the British Library

ISBN 1–874350–37–X

Produced by Wessex Archaeology
Printed by Cromwell Press Ltd, Trowbridge

The cost of this publication was met by English Heritage and Historic Scotland

Front cover: main picture: reconstructed buildings at Butser Ancient Farm, Hampshire (© Wessex Archaeology); roundhouse at Haddenham, Cambridgeshire (© Cambridge Archaeological Unit); decorated mount from Balmaclellan, Dumfries & Galloway (© Trustees of the National Museums of Scotland)

Back cover: Iron animal crest from the Capel Garmon, Conwy, firedog (© National Museum of Wales); Early La Tène brooch from Finlaggan, Islay (© Trustees of the National Museums of Scotland); pit alignment at Shorncote, Gloucestershire (© Oxford Archaeological Unit)

Contents

Summary

This paper identifies five strategic areas which are central to future research on the British Iron Age. These are:

- chronological frameworks
- settlement patterns and landscape history
- material culture studies
- regionality, and
- the nature of socio-economic changes during the period.

For each theme, the paper assesses the state of current knowledge and identifies specific research topics and priorities, together with the necessary refinements for collecting and analysing data. A number of areas where changes in archaeological practice would be beneficial are highlighted The survey covers England, Scotland and Wales, but not Ireland. Whilst directed primarily at the pre-Roman Iron Age, many of the points in the paper apply to native settlements inside and outside the Roman province, as well to the later Bronze Age.

Much of the archaeological research which takes place in Britain today is as a result of development. A key aim of this paper is to provide support for local curatorial decisions, ensuring that research opportunities brought about by developer-funding are realised to the full. Universities and museums have a key role, too, in encouraging and facilitating student projects. The existence of an overall framework will, we believe, assist in the development of detailed research strategies at regional level, whilst providing a yardstick against which more local agendas can be measured and refined. Specific action points are summarised at the end of each section; theme by theme, the main research priorities are as follows:

In many regions of Britain, even basic Iron Age chronology is a problem, while most others still rely heavily on a few key sequences or artefact associations. Regional audits should be undertaken to identify weaknesses in the existing chronologies, and multiple single-entity radiocarbon dating needs to become routine for Iron Age sites. Absolute dating strategies should be a requirement of all briefs for developer-funded projects on Iron Age sites, with systematic palaeo-botanical sampling to ensure an adequate choice of single entity samples, as well as providing environmental data. A certain number of strategic and retrospective absolute dating programmes could usefully be developed, whilst the potential of alternative scientific dating methods should be further explored. The importance of any excavated finds of dateable metalwork in closed contexts needs to be highlighted.

The importance of evaluations as a research tool for the study of Iron Age settlement and landscapes needs to be recognised, and the results made more accessible, both locally and nationally. There is urgent need for regional synthesis. Strategies need to be developed for detecting open settlements and burial grounds, and for predicting their locations, whilst project briefs for Iron Age sites need to specify larger and more flexible sampling fractions in order to enable thorough recording and analysis of structured deposits and spatial organisation, as well as making clear the need to look outside visible settlement boundaries, which are often only part of wider 'inhabited zones' where everyday activities took place. In addition, higher levels of quantification and contextual information are required in reports to enable future workers to extract the necessary comparative data.

There is scope for renewed fieldwork and archival research on many published sites, as well as more research on regional differences in Iron Age house organisation and ritual deposits. More work is required on how the different components of Iron Age societies were organised spatially and seasonally across the landscape, and on how Iron Age people understood and perceived their landscapes, and there needs to be greater dialogue between workers focusing on Iron Age societies, and those analysing plants, bones and the environment, in order to tie in agriculture and society. Burials and the surrounding areas require careful excavation to collect evidence for the accompanying rites.

The potential of material culture to contribute to our picture of Iron Age life remains under-exploited. The onus is on specialists and excavators to work together more, and for institutions and funding bodies to encourage a wide rather than a narrow view of artefacts. Recovery, reporting and integration of finds of all types requires basic minimum standards and levels of quantification, whilst scientific analysis is essential, not a luxury. The need for careful study and excavation of 'off-site' artefact deposits and for watching briefs on the dredging of rivers, lakes and coastal waters and drainage of bogs must be emphasised, as must the potential of metal-detector finds to change understandings of the period, an obvious first step being to extend the pilot *Portable Antiquities Recording Scheme* to the rest of the UK. There is an urgent need to train more Iron Age material culture specialists, and to undertake a range of basic artefact studies, corpora, and syntheses, to provide the basis for future identifications and interpretations. More research is needed on primary production sites of all kinds, on the use of various artefact types and materials, and on the distribution of the finished products.

Over the last decade, it has become increasingly clear that regional variations are a central feature of the British Iron Age, and defining and evaluating these differences should be a core objective of future research. Efforts are also needed to correct the substantial variations in knowledge that currently exist between different parts of Britain, since these seriously distort our understanding of the period. Some areas are still effectively blank, and in these, any opportunities for fieldwork on Iron Age sites should be treated as potentially significant for advancing understanding at national level. Many other regions would benefit from synthesis and from projects aimed at filling gaps in the existing framework.

Compared to the later part of the period, the earlier Iron Age emerges as poorly understood. In the present state of knowledge, all sites of this period, however ephemeral, have a high research priority. Excavation of a range of settlement types and landscape features is needed in all areas, as is research on regional pottery sequences, supported by absolute dating programmes. Further investigation of the contexts of late Bronze Age and early Iron Age metalwork is vital to understanding the changing roles of these objects and should include consideration of their wider landscape setting, as well as the excavation of discovery sites. The organisation, location and scale of early iron production and its relationship to other technologies (including flint) are also high priorities for research.

More precise chronologies are essential to understand the rate, scale and cause of economic and social changes during the later Iron Age, implying routine use of absolute dating on sites of the period. Two topics requiring particular attention are the nature of the archaeological transition from the earlier Iron Age, and the cause and consequences of settlement expansion in different regions of Britain after *c.* 300 BC. New models need to be developed to explain archaeological changes in southern and eastern England during the last two centuries of the period, whilst the increased abundance of finds on later Iron Age sites, and the contemporary changes in the organisation, intensity and scale of agricultural and craft production require detailed local investigation and inter-regional comparison. Further research is needed into the nature and degree of later Iron Age changes in parts of Britain outside the south-east.

Membership of the working party:

C. Haselgrove (Convenor) (Department of Archaeology, University of Durham)

I. Armit (Department of Archaeology, Queen's University, Belfast)

T. Champion (Department of Archaeology, University of Southampton)

J. Creighton (Department of Archaeology, University of Reading)

A. Gwilt (Department of Archaeology, National Museums and Galleries of Wales, Cardiff)

J.D. Hill (Department of Prehistory and Early Europe, British Museum, London)

F. Hunter (Department of Archaeology, National Museums of Scotland, Edinburgh)

A. Woodward (Birmingham University Field Archaeology Unit).

Acknowledgements

The working party wish to thank everyone who commented on the draft report, as well as all the individuals and organisations who provided illustrations for use in the final publication.

Zusammenfassung

Dieser Artikel bestimmt folgende fünf strategische Gebiete, die für die zukünftige Erforschung der britischen Eisenzeit von zentraler Bedeutung sein werden:

- Chronologisches Gerüst
- Siedlungsformen und Landschaftsgeschichte
- Studien zur materiellen Kultur
- Regionalität und
- Art der sozio-ökonomischen Veränderungen während dieser Zeitperiode

Für jedes dieser Themen wertet der Artikel den aktuellen Forschungsstand aus und identifiziert sowohl die spezifischen Forschungsthemen und Forschungsschwerpunkte als auch die notwendigen Verfeinerungen für die Aufnahme und die Analyse der Daten. Dabei werden eine Reihe von Gebieten festgestellt, in denen eine Änderung der archäologischen Praxis von Vorteil wäre. Die Untersuchung umfaßt England, Schottland und Wales, aber nicht Irland. Obwohl er primär auf die vorrömische Eisenzeit ausgerichtet ist, treffen viele Argumente und Gesichtspunkte, die im Artikel beschreiben werden, auch auf die einheimischen Siedlungen, die sich sowohl in als auch außerhalb der römischen Provinz befinden, genauso zu, wie auf die späte Bronzezeit.

Ein großer Teil der archäologischen Forschung, die heute in Britannien stattfindet, ist das Ergebnis von Baumaßnahmen. Ein Hauptziel dieses Artikels ist es, eine Hilfestellung für lokale denkmalpflegerische Entscheidungen zu geben, die sicherstellt, daß die Forschungsmöglichkeiten, die sich durch die Finanzierung eines Bauherrn ergeben, voll und ganz erkannt werden. Universitäten und Museen kommt dabei eine Schlüsselrolle zu, indem sie studentische Projekte fördern und unterstützen. Wir glauben, daß die Schaffung eines übergeordneten Rahmens bei der Entwicklung von detaillierten Forschungsstrategien auch auf der regionalen Ebene hilft, indem er einen Maßstab liefert, an dem lokale Vorhaben gemessen und verbessert werden können. Spezifische Aktionspunkte werden am Ende jedes Abschnitts zusammengefaßt; die Forschungsschwerpunkte sind nach Themen wie folgt geordnet:

In vielen Regionen Großbritanniens ist selbst die grundlegendste Chronologie der Eisenzeit ein Problem, während sie in anderen Regionen immer noch hauptsächlich auf einigen wenigen Kernsequenzen von Artefakt - Assoziation fußt. Deshalb sollten regionale Überprüfungen durchgeführt werden, um die Schwächen der bestehenden Chronologiesysteme ausmachen zu können. Zudem müßten routinemäßig bei eisenzeitlichen Fundstellen mehrfache C14-Datierungen von Einzelobjekten unternommen werden. Die Durchführung absoluter Datierungen sollte eine Grundvoraussetzung bei allen vom Bauherrn finanzierten Projekte zu Fundstellen der Eisenzeit sein. Zusätzlich sollten systematische paläobotanische Stichprobenuntersuchungen eingeschlossen werden, damit eine repräsentative Auswahl von Einzelproben und Umweltdaten erreicht werden kann. Es könnten eine bestimmte Anzahl an Programmen zur strategischen und retrospektiven absoluten Datierung entwickelt werden, und das Potenzial alternativer wissenschaftlicher Datierungsmethoden sollte weiter erforscht werden. Dabei muß die Bedeutung jedes ausgegrabenen, geschlossenen Fundkomplexes mit datierbaren Metallgegenständen herausgestellt werden.

Auch die Bedeutung von Evaluierungen als Hilfsmittel bei der Erforschung eisenzeitlicher Siedlungen und Landschaften muß erkannt, und die Ergebnisse auf lokaler und nationaler Ebene besser zugänglich gemacht werden, wobei auch eine regionale Synthese unbedingt erforderlich ist. Es sollten zudem Strategien entwickelt werden, mit denen man offene Siedlungen und Friedhöfe erkennen und ihre genaue Lage besser bestimmen kann. Bei Projekten zu eisenzeitlichen Fundstellen sollten größere und flexiblere Stichproben unternommen werden, damit eine sorgfältige Aufnahme und Analyse von strukturierten Schichten und deren räumlichen Organisation möglich ist. Wichtig ist auch, die Untersuchungen über die sichtbaren Siedlungsgrenzen hinaus fortzuführen, da die eigentlichen Siedlungen oft nur ein Bestandteil größerer „bewohnter Zonen" sind, in denen sich das alltägliche Leben abspielte. Daneben sind in den Grabungsberichten anspruchsvollere Quantifizierung und kontextuelle Informationen erforderlich, damit die notwendigen Vergleichsdaten auch zukünftigen Bearbeiter zugänglich sind.

Bei vielen schon publizierten Fundstellen gibt es Handlungsspielraum für erneute Feldarbeit, Archivforschung und für die Untersuchung regionaler Unterschiede bei Hausbau und ritueller Deponierung in der Eisenzeit. Ein weiteres Arbeitsfeld ist die eisenzeitliche Landschaft, wobei verschiedene Komponenten zu klären sind: Wie organisierten sich die eisenzeitlichen Gesellschaften räumlich und saisonal innerhalb der Landschaft, und wie haben sie ihre Landschaften verstanden und wahrgenommen. Damit Aussagen zur Umwelt und Gesellschaft getroffen werden können, ist darauf zu achten, daß ein intensiverer Dialog zwischen den Bearbeitern entsteht, die sich auf Fragen der eisenzeitlichen Gesellschaft konzentrieren, und denjenigen, die sich vornehmlich mit Pflanzen, Knochen und der Umwelt beschäftigen. Die unmittelbare Umgebung von Gräbern erfordert eine gleichermaßen sorgfältige Ausgrabung wie die Gräber selbst, damit Nachweise für begleitende Riten erkannt und aufgenommen werden können.

Das Potenzial der materiellen Kultur als wichtige Quelle zum Verständnis des Lebens in der Eisenzeit ist noch nicht voll ausgeschöpft. Spezialisten und Ausgräber sind dazu verpflichtet, besser und intensiver zusammen zu arbeiten. Doch auch die Institutionen und Geldgeber sollten eine intensivere Beschäftigung mit den Artefakten fördern. Die Bergung, Dokumentation und Integration aller Fundgattungen erfordert grundlegende Minimalstandards und -ansprüche der Quantifizierung, wobei die wissenschaftliche Analyse aber unentbehrlich bleibt und keinen Luxus darstellen sollte. Die Notwendigkeit einer sorgfältigen Sichtung und Ausgrabung von Niederlegungen von Artefakten außerhalb von Fundstellen, und das Beobachten von Baggerarbeiten in Flüssen, Seen und Küstengewässern sowie bei Entwässerungen von Mooren muß wieder stärker in den Vordergrund gestellt werden. So sollte auch das Potenzial von Funden, die mit einem Metalldetektor gemacht wurden, überdacht werden, da auch sie unser Verständnis einer Periode verändern können. Dabei würde es naheliegen, als ersten Schritt das Pilot Portable Antiquities Recording Scheme auf den Rest des Vereinigten Königreiches auszudehnen. Es besteht eine dringende Notwendigkeit, daß mehr Spezialisten zur materiellen Kultur der Eisenzeit ausgebildet werden. Weiterhin sollten eine Reihe von grundlegenden Materialstudien, Sammlungen und Synthesen durchgeführt werden, um eine solide Basis für zukünftige Bestimmungen und Interpretationen zu liefern. Die Erforschung von primären Produktionsstellen verschiedenster Art sollte verstärkt werden, und dabei sowohl die Nutzung verschiedener Artefaktentypen und Materialien als auch die Verbreitung von Fertigprodukten untersucht werden. In den letzten zehn Jahren wurde zunehmend deutlich, daß regionale Variationen ein zentrales Merkmal der britischen Eisenzeit sind und daß es somit ein Kernziel zukünftiger Forschung sein sollte, diese Unterschiede zu definieren und zu bewerten. Zudem sollte versucht werden den substantiell unterschiedlichen Forschungsstand, der in den verschiedenen Teilen Britanniens besteht, zu korrigieren, da dadurch unser Verständnis dieser Periode beträchtlich erschwert wird. Einige Gebiete sind gewissermaßen immer noch weiße Flecken und hier sollte jede Möglichkeit der Feldarbeit an Fundstellen der Eisenzeit, auch im Hinblick auf unsere Kenntnis auf nationaler Ebene, als wichtig eingestuft werden. In vielen anderen Regionen wären Synthesen und Projekte notwendig, die darauf abzielen, diese Lücken in dem existierenden Gerüst zu füllen.

Verglichen mit dem späteren Abschnitt des Zeitraumes stellt sich die frühe Eisenzeit als eine Periode dar, über die man bisher nur wenig weiß. Beim jetzigen Forschungsstand haben alle Fundstellen dieser Periode, wenn sie auch nur kurzzeitig belegt waren, höchste Forschungspriorität. Ausgrabungen von verschiedenen Siedlungs- und Landschaftsformen sind in allen Gebieten erforderlich. Dasselbe gilt für die Erforschung regionaler Keramiksequenzen, die von Programmen zur absoluten Datierung begleitet werden sollten. Weitere Untersuchungen zum Kontext von spätbronzezeitlichen und früheisenzeitlichen Metallhandwerk sind für das Verständnis der sich verändernden Rolle der Metallobjekte von entscheidender Bedeutung, und sollten deshalb auch auf ihre Verbreitung in der Landschaft hin untersucht werden. Die Ausgrabung von neu entdeckten Fundstellen sollte ebenfalls verstärkt betrieben werden. Die Organisation, Lage und Ausmaß der frühen Eisenproduktion und ihrer Beziehung zu anderen Technologien (inklusive Feuerstein) sind auch ein wichtiger Forschungsschwerpunkt.

Präzisere Chronologien sind aber immer noch unentbehrlich für das Verständnis von Anzahl, Ausmaß und Grund ökonomischer und sozialer Veränderungen während der späteren Eisenzeit, was den Gebrauch von absoluter Datierung der Fundstellen der Periode zur Routine werden lassen muß. Zwei Themen, die besondere Aufmerksamkeit erfordern, sind die Art des archäologischen Übergangs von der frühen Eisenzeit und die Ursache und Auswirkung der Siedlungsexpansion in den verschiedenen Regionen Britanniens nach ca. 300 v.Chr. Es müßten neue Modelle entwickelt werden, um die archäologischen Veränderungen im südlichen und östlichen England während der letzten zwei Jahrhunderte dieser Periode zu erklären, während die zunehmende Menge an Funden aus Fundstellen der späteren Eisenzeit und die gleichzeitigen Veränderungen in der Organisation, Intensität und Ausmaß der Landwirtschafts- und Handwerksproduktion detaillierte lokale Untersuchungen und interregionale Vergleiche erfordern. Schließlich werden weitere Forschungen zur Art und zum Ausmaß der Veränderungen in der späteren Eisenzeit in anderen Teilen Britanniens außerhalb des Südostens benötigt.

Peter Biehl

Résumé

Cette étude identifie cinq secteurs stratégiques qui sont au centre des futures recherches sur l'âge du fer en Grande-Bretagne.
Ce sont les suivants:

- Référentiel d'étalonnage chronologique
- Types d'occupation et histoire du paysage
- Étude de la culture matérielle
- Spécificités régionales et
- Nature des changements socio-économiques pendant cette période

Pour chacun de ces thèmes, cette étude évalue l'état des connaissances actuelles et identifie des sujets et des priorités de recherches spécifiques, ainsi que les raffinements nécessaires à la collecte et à l'analyse des données. On attire l'attention sur un certain nombre de secteurs dans lesquels des changements dans les méthodes de travail archéologique seraient bénéfiques. Cette étude couvre l'Angleterre, l'Ecosse et le Pays de Galles, mais pas l'Irlande. Tout en étant, en premier lieu dirigés vers l'âge du fer pré-romain, bien des points dans cette étude s'appliquent également aux occupations indigènes, aussi bien à l'intérieur qu'à l'extérieur de la province romaine, ainsi qu'à la fin de l'âge du bronze.

La majeure partie des recherches archéologiques menées en Grande-Bretagne de nos jours sont la conséquence de travaux de construction. Un des buts clés de cette étude consiste à fournir une forme de soutien pour les décisions de conservation au niveau local, s'assurant que toute opportunité de recherches, suite à l'aide financière d'un promoteur, est saisie et menée à bien. Universités et musées ont également un rôle clé à jouer en encourageant et facilitant les travaux des étudiants. L'existence d'un référentiel global, favorisera, à notre avis, le développement de stratégies de recherche détaillées au niveau régional, tout en fournissant un système de références par rapport auquel d'autres plans d'action locaux pourront se mesurer et s'affiner. A la fin de chaque section, nous résumons des points d'action spécifiques ; thème par thème, les principales priorités en matière de recherche sont les suivantes:

Dans bien des régions en Grande-Bretagne, même la chronologie fondamentale de l'âge du fer est un problème, tandis que dans la plupart des autres, elle repose encore lourdement sur quelques séquences clés ou des associations d'artefacts. On devrait entreprendre des vérifications régionales pour identifier les points faibles dans les chronologies existantes, et la multiple datation au radio-carbone d'une entité unique doit devenir routine pour les sites de l'âge du fer. Des stratégies de datation absolue devraient être exigées de tous les projets d'étude de sites de l'âge du fer financés par des promoteurs, avec une prise systématique d'échantillons paléo-botaniques pour s'assurer d'un choix adéquat d'échantillons d'une seule entité, ainsi que pour fournir des données environnementales. Il pourrait être utile de développer un certain nombre de programmes de datation absolue stratégiques et rétrospectifs, tandis qu'on devrait poursuivre les recherches sur d'éventuelles nouvelles méthodes scientifiques de datation. On doit souligner l'importance des trouvailles de métallurgie datable mises à jour dans des contextes clos.

Il faut reconnaitre l'importance des évaluations comme outils de recherche pour l'étude des occupations et du paysage de l'âge du fer et on doit faciliter l'accès à leurs résultats, aussi bien au niveau local que national. Il existe un besoin urgent de synthèse régionale. Il faut développer des stratégies permettant de détecter les occupations ouvertes et les lieux d'inhumation, et de prédire leurs emplacements, tandis que les dossiers de projets de recherches concernant les sites de l'âge du fer doivent spécifier des fractions d'échantillonage plus étendues et plus flexibles afin de permettre un répertoriage et une analyse approfondis des dépôts structurés et de l'organisation spatiale, tout en insistant sur la nécessité de regarder à l'extérieur des limites visibles de l'occupation, qui ne constituent souvent qu'une partie de 'zones habitées' plus étendues où se déroulaient un certain nombre d'activités quotidiennes. De plus, nous avons besoin d'un plus grand nombre de renseignements quantitatifs et contextuels pour permettre aux futurs chercheurs d'en extraire les données comparatives nécessaires.

Il existe des possibilités pour de nouvelles recherches, soit par arpentage, soit grâce aux archives sur beaucoup de sites qui ont déjà fait l'objet de publications, ainsi que pour des recherches supplémentaires sur les différences régionales dans l'organisation de la maison et les dépôts rituels à l'âge du fer. Il y a encore du travail à fournir sur la façon dont les différents composants des sociétés de l'âge du fer s'organisaient dans l'espace et dans le paysage en fonction des saisons, et sur la manière dont les peuples de l'âge du fer
comprenaient et percevaient leur environnement, et il faut qu'un dialogue plus soutenu s'instaure entre ceux dont le travail se concentre sur les sociétés de l'âge du fer et ceux chargés d'analyser les plantes, les os et l'environnement, afin d'établir des liens entre agriculture et société. Les inhumations et leurs alentours doivent être fouillés avec précaution afin de recueillir des témoignages sur les rituels qui les accompagnent

Le potentiel que possède la culture matérielle de contribuer à notre image de la vie à l'âge du fer reste sous-exploité. C'est à la charge des spécialistes et des fouilleurs de travailler en plus étroite collaboration, et aux institutions et organismes de financement d'encourager une approche d'ensemble plutôt qu'une vue restreinte des artefacts. La récupération, l'enregistrement et l'intégration des trouvailles de tous types exigent des niveaux de base et des degrés de quantification minimum, tandis que l'analyse scientifique est essentielle, pas un luxe. On doit insister sur la nécessité d'étudier et de fouiller soigneusement les dépôts d'artefacts en dehors du site et de surveiller le draguage des rivières, lacs et eaux côtières, et le drainage des marais, tout comme le potentiel de trouvailles par détecteurs de métaux de changer notre compréhension de la pérode, un premier pas évident consisterait à étendre le projet pilote appelé Projet de Répertoriage d'Antiquités Portable au reste du Royaume-Uni. Il est urgent de former davantage de spécialistes en culture matérielle de l'âge du fer, et d'entreprendre diverses études d'artefacts fonda-mentales, corpora et synthèses, afin d'offrir une base pour de futures identifications et interprétations. Nous avons besoin de plus de recherches sur les sites de production primaire de toutes sortes , sur l'utilisation de divers types d'artefacts et de matériaux, et sur la distribution des produits finis.

Au cours de la dernière décennie, il est devenu de plus en plus évident que les variations régionales forment un trait essentiel de l'âge du fer britannique, et définir et évaluer ces différences devrait constituer un des objectifs centraux des recherches à venir. Il est aussi nécessaire de faire des efforts pour corriger les variations substantielles qui existent maintenant dans les connaissances que nous avons des différentes parties de la Grande-Bretagne,car celles-ci déforment sérieuse-ment notre compréhension de cette période. Certaines régions sont en fait encore quasiment vierges, et dans celles-ci on devrait considérer toute opportunité d'arpentage de sites de l'âge du fer comme potentielle-ment significative pour l'avancement de nos connaissances au niveau national. Beaucoup d'autres régions bénéficieraient d'une synthèse et de projets ayant pour but de combler les lacunes dans le cadre existant.

Comparé à la phase finale de cette période, le début de l'âge du fer apparaît comme très mal compris. Dans l'état actuel de nos connaissances tous les sites de cette période, aussi éphémères soient-ils, sont placés très haut sur l'échelle des priorités de recherches. On a besoin de fouiller un certain nombre de types d'occupation et de particularités dans le paysage dans toutes les régions, tout comme sont nécessaires des recherches sur les séquences de poterie régionale, accompagnées de programmes de datation absolue. Des études supplémentaires des contextes de la métallurgie de la fin de l'âge du bronze et du début de l'âge du fer sont indispensables pour comprendre les changements dans le rôle de ces objets et devraient inclure un examen de leur place dans un paysage plus étendu ainsi que la fouille des sites où ils ont été découverts. L'organisation, l'emplacement et la taille de la première production de fer et sa relation avec les autres technologies (y compris le silex) sont également des domaines de recherches prioritaires.

Des chronologies plus précises sont esssentielles pour comprendre l'ampleur, l'échelle et la cause des changements économiques et sociaux pendant la période finale de l'âge du fer, ce qui implique l'utilisation routinière de la datation absolue sur les sites de cette période. Deux aspects qui méritent une attention particulière sont la nature de la transition archéologique du début de l'âge du fer, et la cause et les conséquences de l'expansion des occupations dans diverses régions de Grande-Bretagne après environ 300 av. J.-C..Il faut développer de nouveaux modèles pour expliquer les changements archéologiques dans le sud et l'est de l'Angleterre pendant les deux derniers siècles de cette période, tandis que l'abondance croissante de trouvailles sur les sites de la fin de l'âge du fer, et les changements contemporains dans l'organisation, l'intensité et l'échelle de la production agricole et artisanale exigent des études locales détaillées et des comparaisons inter-régionales. Des recherches supplémentaires doivent être entreprises sur la nature et le degré des changements de la fin de l'âge du fer dans les parties de la Grande-Bretagne autres que le sud-est.

Annie Pritchard

Understanding the British Iron Age:
an Agenda for Action

A. INTRODUCTION

In 1996, English Heritage published *Frameworks for Our Past* (Olivier 1996) in order to encourage the development of regional research strategies covering the whole of England. All sides of the profession see these as essential to provide local authority archaeologists with a framework for making judgements about the relative importance of threatened sites and to maximise the new research opportunities which PPG 16 has created. Since the 1996 initiative, archaeologists in England have been engaged in detailed resource assessments as a preliminary to formulating locally-relevant research frameworks (e.g. Glazebrook 1997) and there have been similar discussions in Scotland and Wales. Whilst significant progress has been made in defining future regional priorities, these discussions have also highlighted the critical issue that no single area can be considered entirely in isolation. The archaeology of each region contributes to a wider spatial and temporal picture, which in turn helps define what is unusual or exceptional about a given region or locality.

The consequent need for national research frameworks and debate to inform regional research strategies and vice-versa is endorsed by English Heritage and Historic Scotland, who have led the way, issuing valuable general statements of their own (Barclay 1997; English Heritage 1998a) – although CADW has yet to produce a similar document for Wales. However, more detailed priorities for specific periods and themes can only emerge from archaeologists working in the relevant subject area, but the foundation which exists for achieving this is very variable. In some areas, like Roman archaeology, a tradition of reviewing research priorities at intervals is already established (e.g. SPRS 1985), and there are specialist societies to sponsor such initiatives. A new agenda for Roman Britain was published earlier this year, based on a day of presentations at the 1999 Roman Archaeology Conference (James and Millett 2001).

In contrast, previous discussion of Iron Age research priorities has generally been within the context of wider reviews, encompassing the whole of British prehistory (e.g. Prehistoric Society 1988). For a detailed statement, we need to go back over 50 years (CBA 1948). A group of us involved in British Iron Age studies decided that the time had come to undertake a detailed review of the subject and to identify key research priorities for Iron Age archaeology in the twenty-first century, as well as suggesting appropriate strategies for taking these forward at local, regional and national level. This plan was endorsed at an Iron Age Research Seminar held in Cardiff in 1997 and the following year, an early draft of the present paper was discussed at a second seminar in Sheffield to which both specialists and non-specialists were invited. The present text owes much to the detailed comments made by other participants during and after the Sheffield meeting. An electronic version of the paper was posted on the web early in 2000 and further comments invited by email for incorporation in this final draft. (URL: http://www.reading.ac.uk/~lascretn/IAAgenda.htm)

A key aim of this paper is to provide support for local curatorial decisions. Since PPG 16 was introduced most excavations on Iron Age sites have been as a result of development and this state of affairs is set to continue, yet the responsibility for recommending what is to be recorded or preserved generally resides with planning archaeologists who are not specialists in the period and who have limited time to keep abreast of research in all the many fields they have to deal with. In recent years, several volumes have appeared which challenge traditional views of Iron Age Britain (e.g. Hill 1995a; Champion and Collis 1996; Gwilt and Haselgrove 1997; Bevan 1999), laying stress on the complexity and diversity of the record created by its inhabitants. We cannot however expect developers to pay for recording threatened sites at the level of detail which these new ideas about the Iron Age demand unless local government archaeologists have been made aware of the relevant issues and provided with supporting justification in a form which they can use to inform the planning process. Of course, ensuring

Fisher's Road, Port Seton, East Lothian: excavation of Iron Age roundhouse and enclosed settlement in advance of housing development (© C. Haselgrove)

Goldcliff, Severn Estuary: rectangular building 6, dendrochronologically dated to spring 273 BC, exposed on peat surface in the intertidal zone (Photo: L. Bolton, © Goldcliff Project)

that rescue excavations contribute the maximum amount of new knowledge is only one aspect of research; giving new meaning to existing data and exploiting the mass of Iron Age material which already lies in museums and excavation stores are just as important.

The paper focuses on five themes which stand out as being of particular importance as Iron Age studies stand today. These are

- chronological frameworks;
- settlement patterns and landscape history;
- material culture studies;
- regionality; and
- socio-economic changes during the period.

For each of these strategic themes, we assess the state of current knowledge and seek to identify specific research topics and priorities, together with necessary refinements for collecting and analysing data. We make no claim to cover every potentially relevant question. As James and Millett (2001, 2) note, a useful agenda can only really be defined for topics which are to some extent predictable. We have concentrated on the building blocks and have not, for example, discussed problems with the models used in interpreting Iron Age societies, although a lack of concern in the last 15 years with the 'big' theoretical issues of Iron Age social structure and political institutions has been noticeable. Other topical areas of enquiry which we have yet to see debated extensively in British Iron Age studies include gender and ethnic identity (cf James 1999). The potential of coastal and maritime archaeology for the period must not be ignored either, as the important results of recent fieldwork in the intertidal zone of the Severn Estuary show (Bell *et al.* 2000).

Each section concludes with a summary of priorities and recommendations. These should not however be seen as prescriptive, any more than we would claim that

they are comprehensive. As already stated, one of our principal aims is to ensure that best advantage is obtained from archaeological interventions necessitated by development by drawing attention to significant gaps in current understanding. Another purpose is to promote better awareness of the richness and diversity of the surviving Iron Age record and to highlight the research opportunities that exist, as well as identifying some problems that need to be overcome. In this way, we hope to involve as many people as possible in ongoing debate about the period and to stimulate new work which sooner or later will come to challenge many of the 'orthodoxies' set out here.

Our discussion covers England, Scotland and Wales, but not Ireland, and is primarily directed at the period between the eighth century BC when iron first came into common use in the British Isles (Needham *et al.* 1998) and the first century AD, although many of the points made here apply with equal force to Roman Iron Age communities outside – and indeed inside the Roman province (cf James and Millett 2001) – as well to the later Bronze Age. In order to underpin the analysis presented here, a numerical breakdown of publications on the British Iron Age over the last decade is included at the end of the paper (Appendix). The period is well served with accounts aimed at the general reader (e.g. Cunliffe 1995a; Armit 1997; James and Rigby 1997); the principal work of reference remains Cunliffe (1991).

B. CHRONOLOGICAL ISSUES

B1 *Problems with existing chronologies*

With the arguable exception of Wessex and parts of south-east England, there is no part of Britain where the Iron Age chronological framework is understood in more than outline terms. For many regions even this would be an overstatement, and for some there is no Iron Age chronology at all. Without some chronological backbone, interpretations of the Iron Age beyond the more intensively studied areas cannot progress. Even in regions which have seen much modern work, such as Atlantic Scotland, interpretations are riddled with chronological uncertainties.

In many areas of Britain, we are faced with a profusion of sites and site types which we believe to be Iron Age, often on the basis of limited and potentially ill-founded parallels with sites in other regions, but where there is a total absence of any internal dating framework. A prime example is south-east Perthshire where intensive ground survey and aerial photography has produced a dense distribution of putative Iron Age sites, but where whole categories of monument (e.g. the interrupted ring-ditches, thought to relate in some way to both ring-ditch houses and souterrains) are entirely undated. Other major classes of site, such as the Cornish rounds or the duns of Argyll, can be broadly defined as Iron Age settlement types, but lack sound internal chronologies.

Even in artefact 'rich' areas like Wessex and south-east England, we often overlook how dependent the absolute dating is on a few key sequences and diagnostic artefact types. The existing, essentially ceramic-based, chronology relies heavily on the proposition that broadly similar regional assemblages were in use at the same time. The only thoroughly independently dated sequence is that from Danebury (Cunliffe 1995b), but this only begins in the early fifth century BC and the existence of one entire ceramic phase (cp 6) is still a subject of some contention. Supporting this framework are some 40 usefully stratified brooches and 60 radiocarbon dated assemblages from other sites. The numbers sound satisfactory enough, until the evidence is analysed region by region. Even if we are correct that similar style-zones were broadly contemporary *most* of the time, what of the exceptions where change in one region does not follow another? Identifying such disjunctions is important if we wish to analyse inter-regional relationships with any degree of subtlety, but must start from independently constructed local chronologies (e.g. Knight forthcoming) if we are to avoid circular arguments. The apparent persistence of handmade 'middle Iron Age' pottery traditions into the Roman period in parts of southern and eastern England, without an intervening 'late Iron Age' phase defined by wheelmade pottery, affords a good illustration of this point.

Past typological assumptions inescapably pervade modern interpretations of chronology and sequence with the result that schemes founded on different categories of artefact are often difficult to reconcile. The divergence between the brooch and pottery dating for the King Harry Lane, St Albans, cemetery has received particular attention (e.g. Mackreth 1994), since it directly affects the interpretation of the burial rituals, but many settlement assemblages display similar problems. Potentially crucial correlations with the European material also need to be addressed, as this is one of the major sources of the absolute dates used in Britain. The consequences of the earlier dating for continental La Tène D1–D2 are still being assimilated, but the implications for insular late Iron Age chronology are considerable (Haselgrove 1997, 56–58): evidently cremation was established in parts of southern England before the mid first century BC (Fitzpatrick 1997a), whilst the adoption of other Aylesford-Swarling traits was probably a long drawn out and selective process. An earlier dating for the inception of the East Yorkshire Arras burial tradition has also been gaining ground in recent years, although this is due more to a shift in intellectual fashion over

how quickly typological innovations could travel than to new data (Collis 1994). Issues relating to the adoption of new artefact types and the spread of ideas among European communities cannot be adequately addressed without an independent dating framework.

Chronological issues are also treated differently across Britain. In Scotland, it is common to view the Iron Age as part of a much longer period of development than is traditional further south, with the 'long Iron Age' being seen to continue until at least the Norse incursions. This trend towards integrated study across inherited chronological boundaries is epitomised by the founding of the First Millennia Studies Group as a forum for discussing Scottish archaeology between 1000 BC–AD 1000. The interlude of interaction with the Roman army is increasingly seen as insufficient reason to suspend study after the first century AD, given the manifest continuity of Roman and post-Roman Iron Age communities from their predecessors. Similar arguments for continuity between certain late Bronze Age practices and the early Iron Age in southern Britain (cf Champion 1999) have led many to argue that the first millennium BC, rather than the Iron Age is a more appropriate unit of study. In Wales, however, the traditional Iron Age and Roman divide has tended to remain in place, although the situation in many areas between the first and fourth centuries AD was evidently not dissimilar to that in southern Scotland.

B2 Developing dating frameworks

Building reliable chronological frameworks is a long-term process, and necessitates the adoption of best practice across Britain. Even aspects of Iron Age chronology which we think we understand, for example certain aspects of pottery sequences in southern England, should not be exempt from such examination. The following section outlines a number of steps, not necessarily sequential, which might allow us to improve our chronological interpretation.

B2.1 Dating audit
A first step should be a detailed audit of the existing chronological frameworks on a region by region basis (or thematically, for example by site type). This should encompass not only the existing database of radiometric dates, but also artefact typologies, presumed structural sequences, and the other factors which underpin our present chronological models, in an effort to deconstruct the basis of our existing understanding.

An initial attempt at such an audit for Atlantic Scotland highlighted the pervasive influence of interpretations of the first few radiocarbon dates, made before many of the method's limitations were fully

4

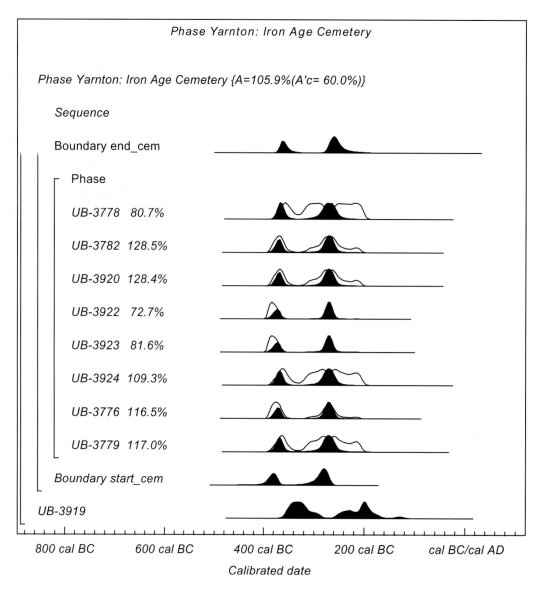

Probability distribution of radiocarbon dates from the Yarnton Iron Age cemetery: each distribution represents the relative probability that an event occurred at a particular time. The distributions plotted in outline are the result of simple radiocarbon calibration. The distributions plotted in black are based on the chronological model used, and illustrate the strong bi-modality present. Other distributions correspond to aspects of the model: the first burial in the group occurring at some time defined as 'start_cem' and the last at the time 'end_cem'. The large square brackets down the left hand side, along with OxCal keywords, define the overall model exactly (Supplied by P. Marshall, English Heritage)

understood (Armit 1991). In the south, the longer chronologies advanced for the South-Western decorated wares and East Midlands Scored Ware rest on an equally small number of determinations (Cunliffe 1991), which might yet be open to re-interpretation. Such an audit can also serve to indicate the areas and site types in most urgent need of secure dating.

B2.2 Scientific dating strategies for fieldwork

The problems of Iron Age chronology across most of Britain make it essential that fieldwork strategies incorporate thorough and thoughtful approaches to the

recovery of chronologically sensitive material. There are several key issues:

B2.2.1 Radiocarbon as routine

Multiple radiocarbon dating must become routine for Iron Age sites, even in southern England. This must be more than tokenism. All excavations should have an appropriate dating strategy from the outset and expect to address the chronological questions to which the site is capable of contributing. This requirement should be built into briefs for developer-funded excavations. Almost all Iron Age sites will yield material suitable for high-precision dating if systematically sampled for carbonised plant remains.

Whilst dating programmes must recognise the problems of the calibration curve between *c*. 800–400 cal BC, we should not over exaggerate them. Using a large enough number of AMS dates and multiple samples can overcome many of the difficulties. Where a suitable stratigraphic sequence exists, application of Bayesian modelling offers significant gains in precision (25–35%) for dating particular events or phases (Bayliss 1998). In many regions, using radiocarbon dating simply to differentiate *earlier* Iron Age sites or occupation phases from those of *later* Iron Age (or late Bronze Age) date would be a major advance.

B2.2.2 Single-entity dating

Establishing sound dating frameworks depends on selecting appropriate samples from reliable contexts. The guidelines issued by Historic Scotland, which promote the use of 'single-entity' dating, should serve as a model for the rest of Britain, limiting the generation of rogue and misleading dates (Ashmore 1999). Essentially single-entity dating means obtaining AMS dates from single pieces of wood, bone or seeds. This avoids 'background' interference from old charcoal which is a persistent (and greatly under-estimated) danger with bulk samples (van der Veen 1992), as well as with timber framed ramparts and other massive timber-structures. Systematic palaeo-botanical sampling during excavation will generally ensure single-entity samples are available from a range of contexts, as well as directly dating crop husbandry practices, whatever their stratigraphic position (e.g. Haselgrove and McCullagh 2000). When dating stratified sequences, finds which are likely to be at their original point of deposition, such as articulated animal bone or dumps of cereal processing waste, are evidently to be preferred (cf Bayliss 1998).

B2.2.3 Organic residues

Recent AMS dating of organic residues on pottery in the Western Isles has provided the first secure dating for settlements of the fourth and third centuries BC (Armit *et al.* forthcoming). Wider use of this technique would make it possible to compare ceramic trends between widely distant geographical areas free from existing assumptions about the direction of influence between them.

B2.2.4 Human remains

Across Britain, a significant number of unfurnished inhumation cemeteries have now been radiocarbon dated to the Iron Age, both in proximity of settlements (e.g. Hill 1982; Parfitt 1995; Hey *et al.* 1999) and in caves (Saville and Hallén 1994), while in Wales, a number of cremations have similarly been dated to the first millennium BC (Williams 1985; Murphy 1992). But for radiocarbon, most of these inhumations and cremations would probably have been attributed to

Middle Iron Age crouched inhumation at Yarnton, Oxfordshire (© Oxford Archaeological Unit)

other periods. Routine dating of unaccompanied burials would enable more thorough exploration of issues surrounding Iron Age funerary practices. Even an absence of Iron Age dates from such a programme would be of value in enhancing the credibility of interpretations based on exposure burial and related rites.

B2.2.5 Reporting of dates

All reports should include critical analyses of the radiocarbon results. It is no longer sufficient or helpful to quote a handful of dates at two sigma. Where appropriate, dates should be combined, using available statistical methods, to give increased precision (albeit with suitable health warnings). This is essential to establish a culture where a critical, but maximising, approach to radiocarbon is a central part of archaeological practice.

B2.2.6 Targeted fieldwork

Targeting fieldwork on poorly dated classes of site, such as the Cornish rounds or the enclosed settlements of the Cheviots, could dramatically improve our chronological understanding. In some areas, excavating and dating a selection of superficially similar cropmark sites may be the only way of differentiating the Iron Age settlement component in a continuum of activity lasting for millennia, as work on the Solway Plain has demonstrated (e.g. Bewley 1994). Once isolated, it may be possible to determine temporally-restricted attributes which would allow the dates to be extended to unexcavated examples by analogy.

Excavation of limited sections of hillfort 'defences' is currently deeply unfashionable. Yet, when a specific threat (rampart-loving rabbits) forced this strategy to be adopted at the Brown Caterthun, the dating evidence accrued transformed our understanding not only of the site, but, by implication, of the Strathmore Iron Age (Dunwell and Strachan forthcoming). Other similar programmes could produce enormous, yet cost-effective, advances in our chronological understanding.

Unfinished wooden bowl, antiquarian find from Kirk-christ, Wigtownshire, radiocarbon dated to c. 70–250 cal AD (© Trustees of the National Museums of Scotland)

B2.3 'Retrospective' dating programmes
While establishing sound dating practice in future fieldwork is an absolute priority, we should also be addressing the potential of existing collections and key sites. Such dating projects could seek research funding through, for example, the British Academy Humanities Small Grants Scheme, the Fund for Applied Archaeological Sciences, or applications to the NERC facility at Oxford.

B2.3.1 The 'art' corpus
It should be possible to 'calibrate' the absolute dating of Iron Age metalwork styles utilising organic elements such as adhering fragments of fabric or mineralised wood, as has been done for late Bronze Age metalwork (Needham *et al.* 1998) and single objects like the Chertsey shield. Bone and wooden objects in museum collections can also be dated, sometimes with un-expected results (Sheridan 1996). The recent dating of animal bone from the famous votive metalwork deposit at Llyn Cerrig Bach, Anglesey, to the fourth to second centuries cal BC has shed valuable new light on the longevity of ritual practices at this site (Hedges *et al.* 1998).

B2.3.2 'Classic' sites
A related priority is dating material recovered from previous excavations at key sites, or obtained by limited new excavations targeted at producing chronologically sensitive material (e.g. Barber and Crone 1993; Needham and Ambers 1994). Numerous sites could yield valuable new information for a relatively small expenditure of resources: contenders include several leading English, Scottish and Welsh hillforts. With more recent excavations, the means is often already at our disposal in the form of seeds or bones lodged in the site archive.

B2.4. Other absolute methods
Important though radiocarbon is, we must utilise alternative forms of absolute dating more widely – even

if their current use is less than wholly reliable; these include thermoluminesence (TL) dating of pottery and daub; optically-stimulated luminescence (OSL) dating of sediments; archaeomagnetic dating of hearths; and dendrochronology. As well as circumventing the radiocarbon calibration plateau, use of these techniques will eventually greatly expand the range of contexts susceptible to chronological analysis.

TL dating is becoming increasingly more refined and Barnett (2000) has shown its potential for dating first millennium BC ceramics in eastern England. Despite the wide error ranges, the use of multiple determinations from sites and single contexts offers considerable potential for close dating. In the areas where pottery was commonly in use, it should be possible to build up a large enough corpus of dates to estimate the duration of more widespread fabric traditions by statistical means, while even in northern and western Britain, the proportion of Iron Age sites with no pottery at all is much lower than is often asserted (e.g. Willis 1999). It remains essential that wherever possible the dates are anchored in typology.

Dendrochronology has been used at wetland sites such as Fiskerton (Field and Parker Pearson forthcoming) and Goldcliff (Bell *et al.* 2000); at several Scottish crannogs; and for dating the Hasholme boat (e.g. Hillam 1992). It is only a matter of time before Iron Age sites with extensive artefact assemblages as well as suitable timbers for dating come to light. Despite the obstacles encountered, the Somerset lake villages are obvious candidates (Coles and Minnitt 1995). Wetland sites also hold out the promise of combining radiocarbon and tree-ring dating, producing further gains in precision, exemplified by the dating of the waterlogged early Bronze Age timber circle uncovered recently at Holme-next-the Sea in Norfolk (Bayliss *et al.* 1999).

B2.5 Exploiting 'dateable' objects from excavated contexts
The potential importance of diagnostic metal artefacts (brooches, pins, harness, razors, weapons, etc.) found in closed archaeological contexts for helping to reconcile absolute, pottery and metalwork chronologies must be emphasised. Only very rarely are such objects found in direct association with reconstructable pottery forms or scientifically dateable material. Such contexts are of especial importance and need to be recognised as such by excavators and curators.

B3 Implementation

- regional audits should be undertaken to identify weaknesses in existing chronologies.
- multiple single-entity radiocarbon dating should be routine for Iron Age sites; absolute dating

Long-lived banjo enclosure under excavation at Nettlebank Copse, Wherwell, Hampshire (© Danebury Environs Project)

strategies should be a requirement of briefs for developer-funded projects.

- systematic palaeo-botanical sampling should ensure an adequate choice of single-entity samples, as well as providing important environmental data.
- selective strategic and retrospective absolute dating programmes could usefully be developed.
- the potential of alternative scientific dating methods should be further explored.
- the importance of excavated finds of dateable metalwork in closed contexts must be highlighted.

C. SETTLEMENTS, LANDSCAPES AND PEOPLE

C1 Current trends in settlement research

The last two decades have seen the end of an era of large-scale excavation of Iron Age settlements, hillforts

and ritual sites with a dramatic floruit of published reports describing the results. From the Breiddin to Danebury, from Thorpe Thewles and Howe to Gussage All Saints and Fengate, or from Fison Way to Rudston and Westhampnett, a massive array of structural, artefactual and biological data is now available in print and in archive. This data relates to Iron Age people, how they lived in the landscape, and how they died. These large excavations have had three lasting impacts; firstly in terms of making familiar a range of settlement types; secondly through studies of plant and animal remains leading to a revolution in the 1980s in our knowledge of later prehistoric animal and plant husbandry, and, thirdly, through a reinterpretation of the ritual and symbolic aspects of certain key sites, a revolution in the 1990s in how we understand the nature of daily life in the period.

Since PPG16, the number of Iron Age settlements and other sites investigated archaeologically in one form or other (whether by fieldwalking, geophysical survey, evaluation or small-scale excavation) has increased dramatically, although differential pressures

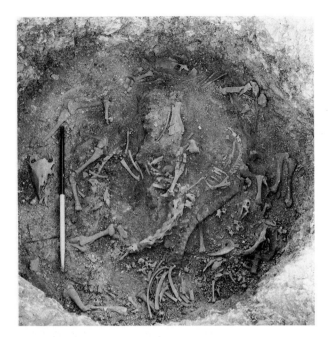

Cadbury Castle, Somerset: middle Iron Age cow burial, found in an area of ritual activity in the centre of the hillfort, near the first century AD shrine (© Somerset County Council)

Suddern Farm Middle Wallop, Hampshire: early Iron Age special deposit in Pit 197 (© Danebury Environs Project)

of development have ensured that this new knowledge is unevenly spread across the country. The approach has been largely site-specific, however, with less concern for wider landscape contexts and settlement patterns. With some exceptions (e.g. Ferrell 1997), there has been little attempt to interpret overall patterns of settlement. Fields have not proved a popular target for study (exceptions include Drewett 1982; Pryor 1996), while compared to earlier prehistory, the symbolic and social aspects of Iron Age landscapes have received more limited attention, although there are exceptions (e.g. Bradley et al. 1994; Bevan 1997; Taylor 1997).

One lasting impact of the excavations in the 1970s and early 1980s was the revolution in our knowledge of Iron Age farming. Key studies of animal and plant remains from Wessex and the Upper Thames Valley were in the forefront of developing these areas of bioarchaeology on a global level (e.g. Grant 1984a; 1984b; Jones 1984; 1985; Maltby 1981; 1985; Wilson 1978), for the first time providing a detailed picture of Iron Age herd composition, age profiles and culling strategies; crop types and husbandry regimes; and coppicing patterns. Significant contributions also came from pollen and soil studies (e.g. Wilson 1983; Robinson 1984; Bell 1996, Tipping 1997), exposing the major intensification of agriculture in the later Iron Age. This work also helped raise issues of wider impact, animal bone studies leading, for example, to the investigation of ritual deposition and the symbolic organisation of settlement space, while palaeo-botanical analysis (e.g. Jones 1984; 1985; van der Veen 1992) provided new ways to consider the large scale

organisation of agricultural systems – and, by extension, the political articulation of social groups – as well as ideas about how specific farming regimes and innovations related to the strategies which family groups employed in competitive social systems. Recent research on Iron Age agriculture is summarised in various papers (e.g. Jones 1996; Maltby 1996; van der Veen and O'Connor 1998), but has yet to be adequately linked with work on social and symbolic aspects of the period.

In the last fifteen years, our approach to interpreting settlement layouts and artefact deposition has significantly altered. In the 1970s, techniques of spatial analysis to define functional activity areas were prevalent, although rarely explicitly employed (e.g. Clarke 1972; Fasham 1985, 127–34). Subsequently, certain workers began to question the very nature of deposition in the Iron Age and to suggest that the layout of settlements was integral to the values and dynamics of the groups who lived in and through them (e.g. Barrett 1989). Work in Atlantic Scotland showed how the syntax of settlement space provided evidence for changes in social organisation (Foster 1989) and has since been extended to consider the monumental (display) and ritual (symbolic) aspects of the Iron Age house (e.g. Armit 1989; Hingley 1992; 1995; Sharples and Parker Pearson 1997).

Equally radical changes have taken place in our understanding of southern British sites. Pit and ditch deposits are no longer seen as random dumps of rubbish (e.g. Cunliffe 1992; Hill 1995a, Chs 8–9; Parker Pearson 1996). Often, contents were deliberately placed, with different artefact types occupying distinct areas of a site, reflecting ideological and cosmological referencing. The orientation and layout of houses is now seen as heavily influenced by cosmology (e.g. Parker Pearson 1996; Fitzpatrick 1997b; Oswald 1997), while the practical functions of the banks and ditches that surrounded Iron Age settlements and hillforts have been questioned (e.g. Bowden and McOmish 1987; Cunliffe and Poole 1991; Hingley 1990; Hill 1995b).

The impact of these studies in transforming our perspective of Iron Age societies cannot be under-estimated. Nonetheless, this work has relied heavily on data from Wessex and Atlantic Scotland, and we need to consider the nature of depositional practices and houses in other regions and through time. Equally, now that ritual and symbolic interpretations are in vogue, it is important to recognise that not everything on an Iron Age site is explicable as 'ritual'. The identification of such aspects always needs to be argued through in detail. In reversing earlier warrior-stereotypes, we must also take care not to de-emphasise completely the possible incidence of conflict and violence in Iron Age societies and to ensure that the potential role of martial ideologies in shaping regional cultural practices and social dynamics receives its due share of attention (e.g. Sharples 1991a).

Future developments include the idea that settlement and landscape space can be viewed in relation to the way the human body moves within that space. This archaeology of 'inhabitation' has been explored in an innovative presentation of the structural and artefactual data from Alcock's excavations at Cadbury Castle, Somerset (Barrett *et al.* 2000). A logical development from these ideas is an analytical approach based on the human senses of sight, hearing, taste, smell and touch like that used on the large settlement excavation at Crick, Northamptonshire (Hughes and Woodward in preparation). Similarly, Giles (2000) has used the abundant evidence from East Yorkshire (e.g. Dent 1982; Stead 1991a), to extend the human body approach beyond the occupation areas to the fields and burial places, opening up possibilities for deciphering the 'inhabitation' of whole landscapes.

C2 Areas for future concern

C2.1 Settlements

Much of the data from settlements excavated before the mid 1990s has been gathered together and discussed at a national, if very general level, in recent surveys of the period (e.g. Hingley 1992; Cunliffe 1995a; Hill 1995c; Armit 1997; Haselgrove 1999a). However, since PPG 16 was launched, keeping informed of evaluations and interventions on Iron Age sites can be very difficult, even in a single county. There is a need for better reporting of all such investigations at both local and national level. At present, the recent survey of later prehistoric pottery assemblages (Morris *et al.* 1998) provides the closest there is to a full database of Iron Age excavations in England. There is also an urgent need for basic regional syntheses. Those which exist for

Wessex (Fitzpatrick and Morris 1994), Essex (Sealey 1997), East Anglia (Bryant 1997) and the East Midlands (Willis forthcoming) stand out as rare jewels. More studies of this kind should be encouraged, as these could act as springboards for policy and research design at the local curatorial level. Iron Age specialists and regional curators also need to work together on developing strategies for detecting 'open' settlements (Haselgrove 1999b). These were probably the domin-ant forms of Iron Age habitation in certain regions (e.g. Hingley 1992) or at particular times, and are probably grossly under-represented in every part of Britain (even in areas where ditched enclosures abound).

It must not be assumed that published sites have been dealt with and 'finished'. Reports are increasingly selective in both content and approach. Vast banks of uninterrogated data lie in museum archives, which need to be continually researched and reassessed in the light of developing theory and new methodologies. Museum collections also contain substantial reposi-tories of unpublished finds and records relating to many key first millennium BC sites, such as Beckford, Ham Hill, Moel-y-Gaer and Mucking. The publication and reassessment of the 1939–40 excavations at Old Oswestry (Hughes 1994) is just one example of what needs to be done. It would also be beneficial to re-evaluate many sites that *were* published between 1935 and 1970. This could be achieved by the selective reworking of artefacts and records, linked to targeted excavations to retrieve specific new data such as environmental remains and samples for dating (as was done in the 1980s at Maiden Castle; Sharples 1991b). The recent investigations on the summit of Traprain Law show what even a relatively small-scale programme of work can achieve (Armit *et al.* 1999; 2000). Other key sites which might profit from fresh work include All Cannings Cross, Little Woodbury, Merthyr Mawr and West Harling, as well as hillforts like Bredon-on-the-Hill or Croft Ambrey.

If their potential for interpreting life in the Iron Age in new and exciting ways is to be realised, sites excavated ahead of development need to be investigated and analysed according to some stringent and novel guidelines, developed in partnership with curators and contractors. Two main areas of innovation are required: first, in relation to sampling fractions as specified in project briefs; and second, regarding the analysis and publication of finds assemblages. In general, sample fractions need to be rather larger and far more flexible than at present. Site briefs should contain suggested sampling fractions for the different types of context expected, ranging for instance from total excavation of graves, preserved floor levels, structural elements of buildings and key placed deposits to lesser fractions for gullies and ditches; the figure of 2% adopted for many field evaluations has no reasoned basis (English Heritage 1998b, Programme

17.1), and is patently inadequate. A suggested minimum for hut gullies and enclosure ditches is 20% evenly spaced around the circuit and this should always include the terminals (Hill forthcoming). Key intersections must be excavated to facilitate site phasing, but as many other segments as possible should be excavated to recover a sufficient number of single-phase context assemblages.

Bulk sampling for botanical remains and sieving for animal bone and artefacts should be routine require-ments in briefs for potential Iron Age sites, supported by scientific techniques such as phosphate analysis, magnetic susceptibility and soil analysis. While the quantities of finds are generally going to look small compared to later periods, maximising their retrieval is essential to define the regionally-specific practices around which Iron Age social relations were evidently articulated. It is also imperative to look beyond visible settlement boundaries (Haselgrove 1999b). At many 'enclosed' sites, pits, structures and even burial areas have been found outside the ditches, while external patterns of deposition (ritual and otherwise) frequently seem to differ from those in the interior. In some cases, ditched enclosures can be shown to form one element of a larger inhabited area, while numerous others constitute phases in a much longer sequence of open and enclosed settlement. There are also indications that the extensive 'open' settlements found in certain areas of eastern England are actually a product of frequent locational shifts by relatively small communities (e.g. Willis 1997; Hill 1999), although some may be genuine nucleated settlements. Non-invasive survey techniques clearly have an important role here, both for planning excavation strategies, and for providing further information about the extent of the inhabited area or variations in the use of space (e.g. Clogg and Ferrell 1991; Bewley 1994; Biggins et al. 1997).

The second key area of innovation concerns the analysis and publication of excavated finds. Discussions of assemblages needs to be more contextual and less compartmentalised into specialist categories than at present (D1.1 below). As well as obvious topics like exchange and interaction with other groups, headings for exploring the data more holistically might include bodily adornment; identity; food and feasting; rubbish deposition; deliberate discard; exchange between groups; and decoration and colour; all of which contribute to our understanding of social and ritual practices. Minimum levels of quantitative and contextual data are essential to allow easier com-parisons of finds assemblages and for others to consider issues of structured deposition and spatial organisation. Above all, the basic finds catalogues need to be properly cross-referenced to information about their phase and context. Such changes, which will affect recording systems as well as post-excavation procedures, have

significant financial implications, but these will be far outweighed by the quality of information gained.

Many briefs and specifications do not currently include explicit project research designs or statements of intent. These are essential for all sites. In cases where large zones of potential first millennium BC landscape are due to be developed, detailed and probably multi-authored research designs must be commissioned. Recent examples of such an approach are the brief for Crick – prepared by Northamptonshire Heritage (the curator) in consultation with a group of academic consultants, and developed by BUFAU (the con-tractor) – and the research design for the new Heathrow Terminal 5 (Andrews and Barrett 1997).

C2.2 Landscapes

To move away from the site-dominated approach of recent decades, we need to develop concepts of landscape which are appropriate to Iron Age studies. The term landscape can be defined at a series of levels. In many reports, the term refers to the natural geographical area within which the site is situated, and is discussed, if at all, in terms of basic environmental and topographic data. In effect, the natural landscape becomes a blank backdrop against which Iron Age life is played out. Social discussions of landscape similarly focus mostly on the degree of management and extent of alteration by human agency, illustrated by dis-tribution maps of nearby settlements, hillforts and fields. But landscape archaeology is much more than this.

Most Iron Age settlements were farmsteads, most Iron Age people were farmers, and farming formed the basis of Iron Age societies. Although archaeo-botanical and archaeo-zoological studies are offering more sophisticated elucidation of Iron Age agricultural regimes and their variation in space and time (e.g. Jones 1996; Hambleton 1999), this work is only loosely articulated with research on other aspects of material culture and society. A more inclusive approach is required, which would transcend the normal separate reports on the animal and plant remains. One answer is to develop an agrarian sociology for the Iron Age. Animals provided meat, but just as important were their roles as draught and pack animals, and as symbolic wealth (cattle and horse); as raw materials for clothing (leather, skins, wool, sinews); as providers of dairy produce and manure (cattle and sheep); and as aids to herding and hunting (dogs). Plants provided staple foods, but also fodder; fuel for the ever-essential fires and ovens; and bedding and roofing material (heather, straw, peat, turf). Managed woodland provided resources for building, fencing and hurdling, wheels and carts. Fields and boundaries were developed in abundance; pasture was maintained within fields and as controlled grazing; both animals and plant products moved around the landscape; and seasonal exploitation has been demonstrated. Such themes need to be welded together to produce a new picture of farming life in the Iron Age. How was the daily work schedule arranged, and how did it vary with the seasonal cycle? How much time was devoted to various crafts and processing activities, and how was labour apportioned by age, class and gender?

We have already stressed the need to think (and excavate) beyond the site. A dynamic sociological approach to Iron Age farming is dependent on detailed understanding of how the landscape around settlements was used. One aspect is mapping and excavating field systems and other boundaries, as well as neighbouring habitation sites. But recent work is recognising an increasing range of 'non-settlement' components of the Iron Age landscape. These include sites with clearly identifiable functions, such as salt production, quarrying, iron smelting and shrines. Others were probably temporary camps and shielings connected with seasonal movements of people and livestock over potentially long distances, like the rectangular buildings excavated at Goldcliff and other sites on the Severn Levels (Bell *et al.* 2000). Yet others comprise isolated wells, shallow pits, or other features with few finds, often ill-defined and usually over-looked, but important evidence for landscape utilisation. These uses of the near and faraway landscapes were all part of the way in which Iron Age peoples perceived and understood their world. The difficulty of identifying which elements are related will be evident, although with GIS this is no longer quite so daunting a challenge as it would once have been; we also need to overcome the conceptual separation which still characterises many wetland projects, where the emphasis is on the wetland to the exclusion of the wider landscape with which it was articulated (*ibid.*, 349).

Symbolic aspects of the landscape need to be considered as well. As several recent studies have shown, the patterns of structured deposition seen on settlements extended across the landscape (e.g. Fitzpatrick 1984; Bradley 1990; Hunter 1997). The placing of weapons and other metalwork in rivers and bogs; the concealment of torcs, harness and coins (singly or in hoards) in dry parts of the landscape; and ritual deposits of pottery and bone in wells or ditches were all important aspects of Iron Age behaviour. It is also clear that there are more Iron Age burials outside settlements than hitherto appreciated, making radiocarbon dating of unaccompanied inhumations essential (B2.2.4 above). Other work has emphasised the importance of earlier monuments as ritual foci and for the laying out of agricultural landscapes (e.g. Hingley 1999; Gillings and Pollard 1999). Greater recognition and more careful study of all these 'off site' activities in their immediate and wider landscape contexts is of vital importance, as is the integration of

Recent excavations on the summit of Traprain Law, East Lothian (© Trustees of the National Museums of Scotland)

this evidence with environmental data in order to understand fully how specific settlements 'worked' in their social landscapes.

In order to achieve a more mature understanding of Iron Age landscapes, the results of new excavations of settlements and other loci of activity – sampled and contextually analysed along the lines recommended above – and data obtained by reworking old assem-blages and archives, need to be combined with the strategic study of fields and boundaries in compact landscape blocks. Such study areas could usefully include the environs of other Wessex hillforts such as St Catherine's Hill to set beside the important results obtained around Cadbury Castle and Maiden Castle, and above all Danebury (Cunliffe 2000; Cunliffe and Poole 2000), where the Environs Project is now in its second phase; an upland farming landscape, perhaps in Northumbria or Wales; a zone on the fringe of Salis-bury Plain; or a river valley and its neighbouring hills – with the report on Conderton Camp now in press (Thomas forthcoming), a promising candidate might be the Bredon Hill forts and the gravel terrace sites like Kemerton and Beckford below. In Scotland, a programme of survey and excavation on cropmark enclosures around Traprain Law has recently started in

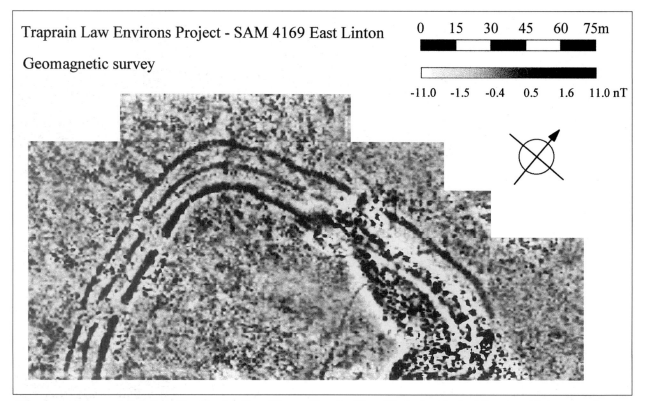

Traprain Law Environs Project - SAM 4169 East Linton

Geomagnetic survey

0 15 30 45 60 75m

-11.0 -1.5 -0.4 0.5 1.6 11.0 nT

Geomagnetic survey of multivallate 'fort' at East Linton, East Lothian (© Archaeological Services, University of Durham)

the East Lothian coastal plain, with the intention of setting the occupation sequence there in its regional context.

Over the last decade, evaluations have become the most important research tool for landscape studies in contemporary archaeology. On their own, the small areas exposed and finds assemblages may seem inconsequential, but imaginatively combined they provide a sample which can be used to plot settlement patterns, human presence and social change across whole landscapes. Yates' (1999) research is a good example of what is possible: working mostly from evaluation reports, he was able to identify a wealth of new Bronze Age field systems in the Thames Valley. Compared to the more intensive excavation strategies recommended above, such projects would be relatively inexpensive, but the research rewards would be far-reaching indeed and would almost certainly transform our current perception of Iron Age settlement and landscape organisation. On a more general level, basic mapping and analysis of the aerial photographic archive, similar to that undertaken by Stoertz (1997) in East Yorkshire or by Whimster (1989, figs 22–28) in the Welsh Marches, remains a pressing need in many areas and would provide a powerful tool for investigating the Iron Age landscape.

C2.3 Burials

Both from settlement excavations and from the recent discovery of several unfurnished inhumation cemeteries

(B2.2.2), it is clear that human remains of Iron Age date – whether individual burials or disarticulated bones – are more frequent than once thought. Although this evidence is very unevenly distributed in time and space and is unlikely ever to be representative of the population as a whole, it is still our most direct point of contact with Iron Age people. As well as providing insights into areas like belief, social structure, wounding in combat, and attitudes to death (e.g. Dent 1983; Parker Pearson 1999), such remains are a prime source of information – over a period of nearly a millennium – about matters such as appearance and stature, genetic makeup, health and mortality rates, and environmental pollution, many of which have an importance beyond archaeology. Biased or not, it is important that any finds of Iron Age human remains are exploited to the full, both in the field and in the laboratory.

Most of the points made regarding the development and implementation of project briefs for settlement investigations and the need for holistic contextual analysis and publication (C2.1 above), apply equally forcefully to mortuary evidence, whether recovered as 'formal' cemeteries, or in other types of context. Where burial grounds are discovered, it is important to look beyond the actual graves, for instance for associated structures or pyre sites which may provide insights into earlier stages of the funerary rituals, as at Westhampnett (e.g. Fitzpatrick 1997a). As this and other recent studies (e.g. Pearce 1997; Parker Pearson 1999) have

Excavating a chariot burial, Newbridge, Midlothian (© Trustees of the National Museums of Scotland)

shown, detailed contextual analysis of body treatment and spatial patterning can reveal a great deal about regional age, sex and status differences, as well as local descent systems and kinship organisation, and the wider cosmological and symbolic principles underlying the relationship between the dead and the living in different parts of Britain.

There is evident need for research into the location of Iron Age burials and how these relate to other components of the settlement pattern. Outside East Yorkshire, where the Arras rite barrows produce readily identifiable cropmarks, Iron Age cemeteries and burial places are difficult to detect and are mostly chance discoveries. In south-east England, as well as in other areas like Cornwall or East Lothian where the numbers of known Iron Age burials have gradually mounted over the years, GIS analysis of their landscape setting might well prove worthwhile. Any patterns which this revealed could be used to predict the zones where Iron Age burials are most likely, so that evaluations could be carried out ahead of development. Other contexts which merit particular attention include settlement boundaries and the vicinities of settlement enclosures; the landscapes within and

14

around earlier Neolithic and Bronze Age monuments, many of which produced evidence of re-use as burial places in the Iron Age (e.g. Warrilow *et al.* 1986; Murphy 1992), and caves (Saville and Hallén 1994).

The potential of DNA analysis for Iron Age populations also needs to be explored. DNA studies ought, for example, eventually to be able to determine if the individuals buried within sites like Danebury were closely related to one another, or genetically hetero-geneous - as might be expected if it was outsiders who received such treatment. Extracting DNA from British and continental burials could provide genetic data relevant to current arguments over the ethnic identity of insular Iron Age peoples (e.g. James 1999), and might help to resolve long standing controversies such as whether or not the Arras burials of East Yorkshire, or the Aylesford burials of south-east England, included a significant immigrant element. It remains to be seen what the evidence from the new female chariot burial at Wetwang Slack, which appears to be early in the chronological sequence, will contribute to this debate.

C3 *Implementation*

- the importance of evaluations as a research tool should be recognised and results made more accessible, locally and nationally. There is urgent need for regional syntheses of the mass of new data which field archaeology is producing.
- the existence of Iron Age open settlements and burial grounds should be anticipated. Strategies need to be developed for detecting such sites and predicting their locations.
- there is scope for renewed fieldwork and archival research on many 'key' published sites.
- further research is required on regional differ-ences in Iron Age house organisation and ritual deposits.
- project briefs for Iron Age settlements need to specify larger and more flexible sampling fractions in order to enable thorough recording and analysis of structured deposits and spatial organisation.
- briefs should make clear the need to look outside visible settlement boundaries, since these may only be part of wider 'inhabited zones' where everyday activities took place.
- higher levels of quantification and contextual information are required in published and unpublished reports to enable future workers to extract the necessary comparative data.
- dialogue is needed between researchers focusing on Iron Age societies, and those analysing plants, bones and the environment, in order to tie in agriculture and society.

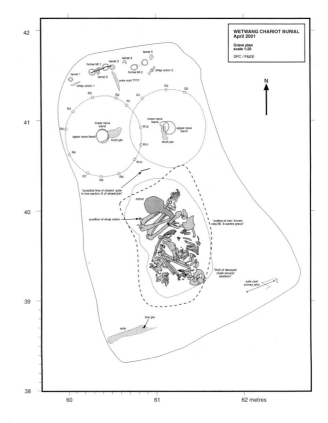

Wetwang, East Yorkshire: plan of the chariot/carriage burial of a woman, interred with an iron mirror (Drawing: S. Crummy, © Trustees of the British Museum)

- more research is required on how the different components of Iron Age societies were organised spatially and seasonally across the landscape.
- in this context, intensive area projects, similar to those already undertaken around some of leading Wessex hillforts, are likely to prove especially valuable.
- we need to consider how Iron Age people understood and perceived their landscapes, in-cluding evidence of relationships with earlier monuments and 'off-site' ritual activities.
- both single burials and cemeteries require careful excavation of not only the graves but also the area around them to collect evidence for the rites that took place.
- the potential of human remains for future anthropological studies should not be neglected. Relating burials to contemporary settlements has rarely been achieved.

D. MATERIAL CULTURE

D1 *General issues*

At its best, Iron Age material culture presents a diversity and complexity unparalleled in prehistory. It

14

is central to increasingly complex interpretations of Iron Age societies, being a prime means to approach topics like status, identity, site function, regionality and relations with Rome. Regional variation in both nature and quantity means that this review can only seek broad trends. It is however axiomatic that best practice in artefact studies can be applied and adapted to a wide variety of situations. The generally larger quantities of artefacts from sites in southern England have led to important research, notably on pottery and coins. However other materials, such as bonework, remain under-studied, while the site-specific nature of many reports inhibits attempts at wider interpretation.

While basic data gathering is by its nature detailed and specialist, the interpretations which can be built on it should be both exciting and contribute to general understanding of the period. We must not forget that in terms of public perception, it is often objects rather than sites which bring the past to life - and therefore justify the archaeological pursuit. This section will first consider data collection and other basic issues of artefact research, before moving on to examine some key aspects of the study of artefact life cycles and priorities for individual material types.

D1.1 Data collection
Clear finds recovery strategies should be established and made explicit in published reports: complex interpretations are unsustainable without well-excavated, quantified data. This needs to operate at various levels. Defined levels of sieving and metal-detecting of spoil should be set, to maximise and standardise artefact recovery. There should also be deliberate targeting of potentially artefact-bearing deposits, for example in the digging of stretches rather than constrained sections of ditches (C2.1 above). When they can be located, production sites remain key targets for investigation, while excavation on finds-rich sites should also be encouraged. Although expensive, this is essential to tackle basic questions such as sequence and chronology, and to provide the quality of data needed for insights into artefact use and deposition – which in turn can provide analogies for less well-preserved sites. The value of waterlogged sites like Glastonbury is clear in this respect (e.g. Coles and Minnitt 1995), while the quality of data from excavations such as Danebury (Cunliffe 1995b) emphasises the value of long term, large-scale projects on artefact-rich sites.

Attempts to define standards for post-excavation analysis, while worthy, are often flawed by a lack of pragmatism and flexibility in their application. However, there is a need at least to recognise minimum standards of recording and publication where specialist groups have defined them, as for example with pottery (PCRG 1995) and the special

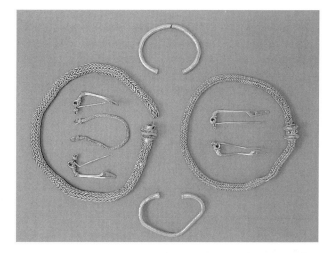

The Winchester hoard, first century BC: gold necklace torcs and other jewellery discovered near Winchester, Hampshire, by a metal detectorist in 2000 (© Trustees of the British Museum)

case of coins (Harrison 1992). For most other materials, there are no accepted standards. This is not a particular problem, provided efforts are made to publicise and expound best practice, as defined by the relevant specialists (D1.2 below).

A key issue is the ability to quantify (C2.1 above). Examples from pottery studies (e.g. Evans 1995) show the great value of simple descriptive statistics for making comparisons and revealing patterns. This does however require data to be easily available from published sources. As microfiche falls from favour there has been a tendency to relegate detailed listings to archive, imposing severe limitations on the subsequent use of the data. If print or fiche is truly unfeasible, then developing technologies such as the Web (e.g. Sharples 1998, 10), CD-ROM or the electronic repository of the Archaeology Data Service (Richards and Robinson 2001; URL: http://www.ads.adhs.ac.uk/projects/goodguides/excavation/) should be used. Paper archives are still required, but electronic archiving provides the potential for access which current archiving policies deny. Improvements in the archiving of the actual material (and the accompanying records) in museums and stores are also essential if future researchers are to make the most of its potential; this clearly has cost implications both for the preparing of archives for deposition and for their long-term curation.

Material culture studies are crucial to site interpretation. The structure of the report is crucial to this. At present, too many reports leave integration of site and artefact data to the user. The ground-breaking report on the Colchester finds showed that a function-based structure was both possible and valuable (Crummy 1983). Whether this is done within or across materials depends on the assemblage involved, as certain categories (such as bone) remain resistant to

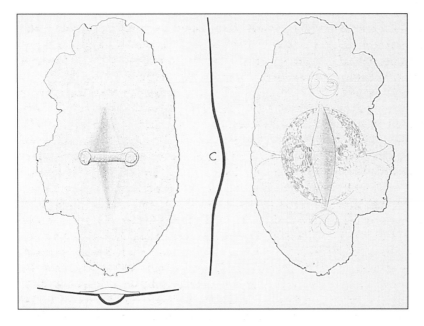

easy functional classification. By involving function, a report is immediately made an active part of site interpretation. It also forces a more holistic view of finds, rather than one compartmentalised between specialisms. The results of using multivariate correspondence analysis to compare Roman assemblages from York (Cool *et al.* 1995) show a promising way forward.

Not all finds arise from excavation. A key consideration in rescue terms is keeping a closer watch on river widening or dredging schemes. Old finds from the Thames, Trent, Witham and Tay show the lurking potential of votive deposits (Fitzpatrick 1984), while work in France illustrates the rewards awaiting focused research (Bonnamour and Dumont 1996). More environmental work on the Holocene development of rivers would be a considerable advantage in predicting where monitoring is best targeted. Similarly, although strategies to deal with the explosion of information produced by metal-detecting are emerging – at least in England and Wales – with the trial introduction of a voluntary reporting scheme, there remains a need for a more proactive role in encouraging finds reporting in many areas. Systematically recorded, metal detector finds have the potential dramatically to change understandings of the period. The recent CBA survey took as one of its detailed case studies the quantitative and qualitative growth in our knowledge of East Anglian coinage, and demonstrated that it was due almost entirely to coins found by metal detectors (Dobinson and Denison 1995). The impact on our understanding of other types of Iron Age metalwork could be just as great.

The first three annual reports of the portable antiquities recording scheme for England (DCMS 1999; 2000; 2001) demonstrate a considerable success in terms of the numbers of objects reported in the trial areas, and the breaking down of mistrust between archaeologists and detectorists, but also indicate the scale of the challenge to be met. The earlier estimate of 400,000 metal-detector finds per annum (Dobinson and Denison 1995) can now be seen as a gross underestimate: a figure in excess of 1,000,000 may be a better approximation. Moreover, the majority of finds which *are* reported remain unpublished. Only with coinage has substantial use been made of the resulting data (e.g. Haselgrove 1987; Curteis 1996). Yet these datasets often represent considerable quantities of largely untapped information, which call into question existing excavation-based pictures of relative Iron Age wealth and poverty. Here, the onus is on all those involved in the recording and identification of portable antiquities and artefacts (national and local museum curators, finds liaison officers, regional and county archaeologists, university staff, etc.) to publish at least a basic record of recent finds. If an excavation backlog is unacceptable, so too is a backlog of finds. Outlets such as *Discovery and Excavation in Scotland* are in-valuable in this respect, as will be the on-line publication scheme for the *Portable Antiquities Recording Scheme* in England and Wales.

In areas where fieldwalking for Iron Age sites is largely futile, as in much of northern and western Britain, metal-detecting can also be a valuable prospection tool, as well as opening avenues to non-normal sites and ritual deposits, which are neither found nor prioritised by conventional approaches. The Salisbury hoard provides a good example of the latter, while highlighting the problems resulting from irresponsible use of metal detectors (Stead 1998).

D1.2 Basic knowledge

For many artefact types, there is a need for basic studies of technology, typology, distribution and dating. A few artefact classes are better studied, primarily coins, decorative metalwork, and in some areas pottery. None are without problems and any investigation will reveal uncertainties, circularity and reliance on often dubious 'fixed points'. In northern England, Scotland and Wales, the presence of Roman finds provides a straight-jacket as much as a framework, pulling dates into a narrow band; in southern England, matters are better, although recent redating of late Iron Age brooches (Haselgrove 1997, 57–58) warns against chronological complacency (B1 above).

The much derided corpus continues to serve an invaluable role as a vehicle of record and a springboard for further research. Many important categories of artefact, however, have not been comprehensively studied for decades, despite the many new finds. The standard work on swords (Piggott 1950) is only now being replaced after 50 years (Stead in preparation), while for pins we must go back to Dunning (1934). Even more recent catalogues such as those for northern decorative metalwork (MacGregor 1976); glass beads (Guido 1978); horse bits (Palk 1984); strap unions (Taylor and Brailsford 1985); and pre-La Tène D brooches (Hull and Hawkes 1987), while invaluable, require updating due to the mass of recent excavation and metal detector finds. Rather than waiting on the vagaries of individual researchers, new databases need to be systematically instigated, perhaps most realistically on a regional basis, and then regularly updated. A possible model is provided by numismatics, which publishes regular round-ups of recent coin finds (e.g. Bateson and Holmes 1997). Specific institutions might perhaps take responsibility for maintaining information on key aspects of material culture, as SMRs do for sites, although this will certainly require additional funding.

There is a pressing need for the relevant specialists to publish articles defining recording standards and research agendas for particular types of material (cf Bishop 1988 on Roman harness fittings). This would encourage wider application of best practice, and help raise awareness of artefactual work, but will require funding, as many of the individuals concerned are freelance. Syntheses are equally essential. Without a comparative framework, artefacts from individual excavations rarely make independent sense. While they may answer questions of chronology and site function, to understand their use and significance requires a wider view. Such surveys provide a context for other workers to interpret their own data, and make it more likely that finds from disparate excavations will be used actively in interpretation. Many catalogues languish as undigested appendices in unremarkable reports. Without synthetic works to assist in making sense of them, their value is limited to an archive one.

The supply of future specialists is a major problem. Material culture no longer figures strongly in undergraduate teaching and there are few MA courses in artefact studies. A lack of career opportunities ensures that few of those who do complete material culture centred PhDs consolidate their expertise into a professional specialisation. Yet many areas rely on a few specialists with no obvious successors. Without enhanced funding it is hard to suggest a way round this problem, although training courses to allow generalists to acquire the basics of a specialisation might be one way forward.

The topic of decorative metalwork exemplifies many of the above problems. This material ought to fuel a wide range of debates – on chronology, continental contacts, hoarding, status, technology and the nature of 'Celtic' art. The long-awaited appearance of *Early Celtic Art in the British Isles* (Jope 2000) finally provides an updated survey of the subject to replace Fox (1958). This is a major and valuable work which will have important repercussions, but the long timescale of its creation and its emphasis on artistic and stylistic aspects mean that it does not furnish the corpus-style database which the subject requires. Individual aspects of art have received thorough treatment (e.g. Stead 1991a; 1995), yet many important metalwork finds are still largely unknown beyond a small and specialist audience. Indeed, even major 'art' objects may be known more by repute than by detailed publication: studies of the Battersea shield (Stead 1985) and the Deskford carnyx (Hunter forthcoming) show just how much new information can be gleaned from such supposedly well-known objects. The detailed re-analysis of the Llyn Cerrig Bach metalwork will similarly augment our knowledge of this major assemblage (Macdonald 2000; forthcoming).

Pottery has fared better, partly because of its abundance and its continuing importance for regional chronologies. Even so, much remains unpublished, including some very important assemblages. In England alone, the recent later prehistoric pottery survey recorded 7138 recognisable pottery collections of first millennium BC date from excavations or fieldwalking at 6977 sites, of which only 2032 (28.5%) are actually published (Morris *et al.* 1998; Morris and Champion 2001). It is evidently desirable that this survey is extended to Scotland and Wales at the earliest opportunity and that steps are taken to reverse this imbalance.

Scientific analysis is still under-utilised. Its value is perhaps best seen in the study of metalwork, where a wide range of established techniques are available. This is one of the few specialist areas to see the development of syntheses and an individual research agenda (e.g. Northover 1987; Dungworth 1996; Bayley 1998). The characterisation of pottery fabrics is the other main area where scientific analysis is routine, and the results often highly informative (e.g. Morris 1994). Similar insights could be expected from many other material types, but often work has not progressed beyond promising initial studies, with little attempt at routine application.

D2 *Artefacts in context*

Artefacts are multi-dimensional objects which can be understood at many different levels. They can provide information about the context and site where they were found, but also contain data about all phases of their life cycle, from production to discard. They may only be comprehensible in terms of wider regional studies; for some objects, it is only an island-wide or European context which provides an appropriate level of analysis. This section considers general topics relating to the life cycles of artefacts, some of which are discussed in more detail in the section on specific resources.

D2.1 Production and distribution

Actual production sites are sadly under-studied, in part because they are often elusive and located 'in the landscape' rather than coinciding with settlements. Research on iron working sites shows their potential (e.g. Crew 1991; Halkon 1997), while excavations on Kimmeridge shale production sites and salterns are good examples of the insights which industrial sites alone can produce (e.g. Sunter and Woodward 1987; Morris 1994, 384–86). They have a value far beyond the local context, touching on much broader questions of exchange and interaction. There is mounting evidence, for instance around the Humber basin (e.g. Foster 1996; Halkon 1997), to suggest that certain productive activities were preferentially located in marginal areas of landscape, whether for cultural or economic reasons (Haselgrove 1989; Sharples 1990). The scale of the mismatch between recorded metal-work types and actual production evidence from Weelsby Avenue, Grimsby – where none of the terret moulds matched known terret types (Foster 1996) – is particularly sobering, and emphasises the importance of locating and researching foundry deposits.

Broad-scale patterns of artefact production have been considered by Morris (1996), although with an inevitable bias to the better-understood material from southern Britain. Yet few detailed regional studies of the organisation of production exist. With many material types, existing data are perfectly adequate for first-level interpretative models which could provide a framework for further study. Metalworking is a good example, as even older excavations typically retrieved at least non-ferrous metalworking evidence. A broad-brush approach can produce valuable models of the organisation of production, as Northover's (1984) work on contrasting cast versus sheet copper alloy produc-tion showed (but see Morris 1996, 54); or Ehrenreich's (1991; 1994) innovative work on the different levels of iron production.

Distribution studies merit more work, having faded from their processual heyday as practitioners became emburdened with post-modern angst over interpretation. This remains an area where artefact study and scientific analysis can play an important role in revealing patterns, whatever interpretation is then put on them. Studies of salt (Morris 1985), iron (Crew 1995) and glass (Henderson 1989a) highlight the potential. Petrological examination of all medium to large (defined regionally) pottery assemblages should

be standard, while pilot studies on materials like jet (e.g. Hunter et al. 1993; Allason-Jones and Jones 1994) show the possibilities of such work for other categories of artefact. Given the explosion of new metalwork finds, distributional analysis ought now to be able to provide some insights into the output of individual workshops or schools (e.g. Cunliffe 1996).

D2.2 Use

The use of many artefacts remains a mystery. This stems in part from practical unfamiliarity with the materials, in part from a modern distance from handcraft processes generally. Yet studies of artefact function have fallen into disfavour. Experimental work has been under-used, despite metallurgical work which has shown its worth (Crewe 1991). Such practical experience should be more readily incorporated in archaeological knowledge, particularly by guiding the efforts of enthusiastic amateurs (cf Bishop and Coulston 1993, 38–41, for Roman military equipment). In some fields, science can provide insights; organic residue analysis of ceramics, for instance, ought by now to be routine (D3.2.2 below). Recent work has also shown that detailed study of the form, size and use of pottery can help us understand the ways foods were stored, prepared and consumed in the Iron Age (e.g. Woodward 1997; Woodward and Blinkhorn 1997; Hill forthcoming; Hill and Braddock forthcoming).

The value of local ethnography is also rarely appreciated (cf Clark 1951). In much of Britain, there are good records of pre-industrial societies: this applies as much to areas like northern England (e.g. Hartley and Ingilby 1990; 1997) as to more traditional ethnographic haunts such as the Northern Isles (Fenton 1978). For instance, the manufacture of post-medieval handmade pottery in Lewis (Cheape 1988) provides instructive parallels for Iron Age pottery production in the area. While ethnographic analogy is an indication of possibilities rather than certainties, local parallels in similar circumstances *may* have far more validity than exotic ones. This is an area calling for interdisciplinary work. We also need to consider the social and symbolic use of artefacts. It is now commonplace that artefacts are best seen as active objects, their meaning varying in different cultural contexts: the increasingly complex interpretations of Roman artefacts in non-Roman contexts highlight this (e.g. Willis 1994; Hill 1997). Only by tackling artefact use with an expectation of complexity and subtlety will better-rounded interpretations emerge.

D2.3 Deposition

Deposition and related taphonomic problems have been a popular topic in Iron Age studies for several years now, as ideas of deliberate deposition with ritual intent have caught on. However, mere identification of

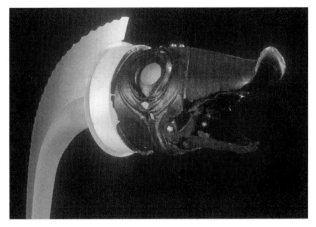

The Deskford Carnyx (© Trustees of the National Museums of Scotland)

Excavation of a votive site at Deskford, Moray where the Deskford Carnyx (right) was found (© Trustees of the National Museums of Scotland)

ritual is insufficient without an attempt to explain it; and concerns with fertility, while undoubtedly important, risk being invoked as a catch-all without adequate exploration.

It is convenient to differentiate on-site and off-site deposition. Apart from opening the eyes of archaeologists to the problem of Iron Age deposition, Hill's (1995a) work on Wessex stands out as an attempt to explain as well as to identify what went on, however tricky this may be. Although similar phenomena have been noted in many parts of Britain (e.g. Hingley 1992; Willis 1999), there are few equally detailed studies (e.g. Gwilt 1997). Yet this is essential, to avoid the uncritical application of a good idea. What happens in areas where pits are less common and preservation less good than Wessex? Regional variation ought to be expected in such rituals. In the Western Isles, for instance, there are recurring deposits of animal bone in houses, but in contrast to Wessex, these often include wild animals (Armit 1996, 155–57).

Much artefact deposition may be structured by guiding cosmological principles, for instance within houses (e.g. Fitzpatrick et al. 1995, 85-89). This shows

the potential of artefacts in tackling complex problems, but equally raises taphonomic issues. The quantities of artefacts involved are often small, and the sites badly plough-damaged. How do such patterns stand up outside Wessex, or on sites with surviving floors, like brochs and wheelhouses (e.g. Parker Pearson and Sharples 1999, 16–21)? While the concept of structured deposition has raised important new issues to be faced in excavations, we need more sites with preserved floor, yard or midden deposits to provide models of 'normal' disposal with which to 'test' the hypothesis (e.g. Needham and Spense 1996; Hodder and Evans forthcoming).

Deposition of artefacts – often valuable metalwork – in the landscape has been studied for some time, with attempts to develop explanatory frameworks (C2.2 above). Despite this interest, few findspots have so far been excavated, although the value of such work is clearly shown by those that have (e.g. Lynn 1977; Stead 1991b, 1998; Fitts et al. 1999). Equally, the widespread use of wet places and other significant natural locations evidently conceals significant regional variations (e.g. Hunter 1997). Votive deposits represent one of the key interfaces between humans and gods, and are crucial to understanding belief systems; if the mechanics of ritual are to be better understood and we are to move beyond pan-Celticism in studies of Iron Age religion (cf Fitzpatrick 1991), investigating regional and chronological variations in the nature and setting of such deposits is essential.

D3 Priorities for particular resources

D3.1 Organic
Organic resources were undoubtedly extensively exploited throughout Iron Age Britain, but suffer from poorer survival than inorganic ones. This leads to them being neglected except in unusual preservation conditions. Material for worthwhile analysis does, how-

	Bone	Textiles	Skins	Wood
Date	X	X	X	X
Function	X			
Technology			X	X
Morphology	X			
Source				

Table 1. Key research areas for organic resources

ever, survive. Evans' (1989) study of decoration, and the division between 'natural' and 'altered' resources, gives an indication of the social insights which can be gleaned even from apparently mundane material. Table 1 sets out some key areas requiring work.

D3.1.1 Bone
All areas are problematic except for technology and source, which can and must be established osteologically. There have been a number of valuable reports (e.g. Sellwood 1984) and syntheses (Foxon 1991; Hallén 1994), but key problems remain, crucially in identifying function (e.g. 'weaving combs'; Hodder and Hedges 1977). Here there is a need for more use of ethnographic analogy (cf Clarke 1971), accompanied by experimental work. The difficulties in identifying the functions of bone (and indeed stone) tools are key obstacles to any attempts to reconstruct lifestyles and differing site functions, as they represent some of the most common but least understood artefacts.

A key point is the sheer quantity of bone. It was one of the most abundant resources in prehistory, and on sites where preservation is favourable is the most abundant find after pottery. This should make us reconsider the apparent poverty of much of the northern Iron Age. A society based largely on organic objects could be highly complex but leave little or no artefactual signal, as a comparison of assemblages from the Western Isles (Hallén 1994) or crannogs (Munro 1882) with those from 'typical' northern sites (e.g. Jobey 1974; Watkins 1980) will indicate.

D3.1.2 Textiles and skins
Both these areas suffer because they are primarily studied by proxy, and fresh insights depend largely on the (essentially serendipitous) discovery of new material. Yet spindle-whorls, loom weights and other tools for textile and skin working are abundant on sites, indicating they were everyday resources. The poor survival of skins raises an important point, suggesting that they were oil-tanned, tawed or smoked, rather than vegetable tanned; compare, for instance, the near total lack of leather from crannogs and other wet sites with the quantity from wet Roman sites. In turn, this implies that the technology for vegetable tanning is a Roman introduction as leather does start to survive in the post-Roman period. For textiles, Bender Jørgensen's (1992,

Wooden paddle, probably for beating flax, antiquarian find from Wigtownshire, recently radiocarbon dated to 770–400 cal BC (© Trustees of the National Museums of Scotland)

120–26) work provides a context into which material can be fitted.

D3.1.3 Wood
Earwood (1993) has shown that the evidence for wood as an artefactual resource is not as poor as once thought, and offers a framework for new finds. Equally, radiocarbon dating has reclaimed for prehistory items previously consigned to post-medieval anonymity (e.g. Earwood 1991; Sheridan 1996). This should be continued and extended to other areas.

D3.2 Inorganic
Inorganic material survives better, and is correspondingly better studied. Areas requiring more work are set out in Table 2 and discussed selectively below.

D3.2.1 Stone
Despite the important work which has already been done, notably on the sourcing and distribution of querns (Hayes *et al.* 1980; Peacock 1987; Heslop 1988), provenance remains an under-researched topic. Many other objects susceptible to provenance studies are sufficiently abundant on sites to yield statistically meaningful data. Recent work on steatite in Scotland has been promising (I. Bray, pers. comm.), while objects made out of materials like jet, cannel coal, lignite and organic shales are all common enough (e.g. Brewster 1963; Hunter 1998a) to merit more attention. Similarly, although certain types of Kimmeridge shale artefact have been studied (e.g. Kennett 1977), no reconstruction of the production system or its extent has been attempted. A campaign of provenance analysis combined with technological and typological study could yield a detailed picture of resource

	Stone	Ceramic	Metal	Glass
Date	X	X	X	X
Function	X	X		
Technology	X		X	X
Morphology	X	X	X	
Source	X	X	X	X

Table 2. Key research areas for inorganic resources

exploitation: Venclova's work in Bohemia (1991) shows the potential.

Function is another key topic, especially for the ubiquitous 'coarse stone tool'. As with bone, these are commonly found but rarely understood. There is need both for regional syntheses to identify recurring types, and for experimental work to clarify function. A related issue is the nature and extent of flint working in the first millennium BC (Ford *et al.* 1984). It needs to be resolved whether late lithic industries similar to those recognised on southern Iron Age sites (e.g. Gardiner 1993) existed in the rest of Britain – as seems likely – and how long these continued (Young and Humphrey 1999). As well as providing a new perspective on later prehistoric technology, defining these industries might, in certain circumstances, provide a means of detecting ploughed-out first millennium BC sites.

D3.2.2 Ceramics

There have been various general reviews of ceramic research (Morris 1994; Woodward and Hill forthcoming) and the PCRG (1995) has already set priorities for research and established minimum standards for recording and publication, while other authors (e.g. Brown 1997; Gwilt 1997; Rigby and Freestone 1997; Willis 1996) have considered technology, typology, distribution, use and meaning. However, relatively little of this work relates to pottery from north of the Humber, despite several studies over the last 20 years which have highlighted the potential of this initially unprepossessing material (e.g. Cool 1982; Swain 1987; Willis 1997); the recent identification of briquetage in north-east England (Willis 1995) is also highly significant. The pottery, including decorated varieties, from the Northern and Western Isles has seen some work (e.g. Topping 1987; Lane 1990), but more is required, for instance on the symbolism of decoration (e.g. Campbell 1991). The other key area is function, where techniques of organic residue analysis have now developed to the extent where useful questions can be tackled (e.g. Heron *et al.* 1991; Dudd and Evershed 1998; Craig *et al.* 2000).

D3.3.3 Metal

Metal is best considered separately as non-ferrous and ferrous. Several studies have shown the potential of copper alloy analysis (e.g. Northover 1984; Dungworth 1996), which should be routine for excavated assemblages. Bayley's work over many years on brooches shows how the gradual accumulation of analyses can be highly significant (e.g. Bayley 1990; Bayley and Butcher 1981). Key questions include a fuller understanding of copper alloy sources – there are hints of patterning (Northover 1984) and the use of local raw materials has been demonstrated in certain areas like north Wales (Musson *et al.* 1992, 277–80),

Burnished later Iron Age pottery vessels from Bramdean, Meare and Old Sleaford (© Trustees of the British Museum)

but many ore sources remain uncharacterised and unstudied. The take-up – or otherwise – of Roman metal (Dungworth 1996; 1997) is another area meriting further study.

Although the study of moulds and crucibles is well-established (e.g. Foster 1980; Bayley 1992), detailed technological examination of objects is less well served, but is crucial to understanding artefacts and their cultural context, for instance the effort required in manufacture, leading on to questions of craft specialisation and patronage. Metalworking is often treated as an intrinsically high-status activity, but in truth we understand little of its detailed meaning or operation, for instance in the role of travelling smiths or the magical aspects of metal (Budd and Taylor 1995; Hingley 1997). As already noted, comprehensive modern databases of major and minor copper alloy objects are urgently needed (D1.2 above).

'Precious' metals are better served: here gold and gold alloys are the main concern, silver being rare to non-existent in most of Britain until a late period in the south. The full publication of the new Snettisham finds will be a major advance, while debate over the date of ribbon torcs indicates there is life beyond East Anglia (Eogan 1983). Warner's (1993) work on gold analyses highlights a topic which merits further study, while the analysis of coin composition is already an area of some success (Cowell 1992; Northover 1992; Hobbs 1996). In general with coins, while practitioners may debate points of detail, there are few obvious lacunae, and the data are increasingly accessible through the web (de Jersey *et al.* 2001). What we need to do now is think, not classify (e.g. Creighton 2000).

Lead is mentioned here as an example of the need to question absence as much as accept presence. In Scotland at least, its presence seems to be primarily an indicator of Roman contact (Hunter 1998b), as Mackie (1982, 71) previously suggested. The same applies to apparently simple items like the iron nail: the main metallic small find on Roman sites, it is all but absent on Iron Age settlements, which in itself speaks of a major cultural difference.

Iron products are in one sense well-studied: there are good site reports and established scientific methodologies, while Scott's (1991) research on a particular region or Fell's (1997; 1998) studies of specific artefact types point to ways to build on the framework we have. Work, however, has concentrated on a few parts of Britain, with others barely touched (e.g. Hutcheson 1997). As with other forms of Iron Age material culture, we should expect regional variation and treat it as a crucial area for study. The reasons for the initial adoption of iron; its roles and abundance; and its great increase towards the end of the Iron Age remain key questions, while the organisation of production also merits further study (F1–F2 below). Crew's (1991) work on the practical side is invaluable, but needs support by equivalent work elsewhere, and by more attention to the by-products of iron working (e.g. McDonnell 1987). Even the basic questions about smelting and smithing activities, such as their technology, location and social interpretation, are poorly understood. Hingley's (1997) foray into the potential symbolism of iron artefacts emphasises the variety of roles which they can play, while Ehrenreich (1994) has linked production to heterarchical forms of social organisation. The divide between practical and theoretical sides of archaeology is well-illustrated here: scientists rarely consider the social use of iron, while many archaeologists do not understand the practical constraints on metalworking.

D3.3.4 Glass

This is one area where substantial understanding has been achieved. Guido (1978) for beads, and Kilbride-Jones (1938) and Stevenson (1956; 1976) for bangles have given us the essential typology – even if dating may, as always, be refined – while Henderson (e.g. 1989b) has, through a sustained programme of analysis, provided a technological framework. Questions, however, remain: notably whether glass was made or merely reworked (Henderson (1989a) argues that evidence for glass-making exists at a number of sites), while the allied topic of later Iron Age red enamels has received little research in recent years despite the increased incidence of enamelled finds from metal detecting (Davis and Gwilt in preparation). The adoption of colours other than red, and their technology, has also seen little study.

D4 Implementation

- The potential of material culture to contribute to our picture of Iron Age life is under-exploited. The onus is on specialists and excavators to work together more and for institutions and funding bodies to encourage a wide rather than narrow view of artefacts.

- Recovery, reporting and integration of excavated finds of all types requires basic minimum standards and levels of quantification. More deposits should be sieved and metal detectors used on the spoil.
- Contributions to site reports should be structured by function, or material and function.
- The careful study and excavation of 'off-site' artefact deposits needs to be emphasised.
- Watching briefs on river-widening; dredging of rivers, lakes and coastal waters; and drainage of bogs are essential.
- The potential of metal-detector finds to change understandings of the period needs to be recognised; initiatives like the *Portable Antiquities Recording Scheme* to encourage better reporting and recording should be extended to the whole of the UK.
- There is an urgent need to train more Iron Age material culture specialists, and to undertake a range of basic artefact studies, corpora, and syntheses, to provide the basis for future identifications and interpretations.
- Scientific analysis of all classes of artefacts is essential, not a luxury.
- More research is needed on primary production sites of all kinds, and on the distribution of finished products.
- Experimentation and local ethnographic analogies may provide insights into the use of various types of artefacts and materials.

E. REGIONALITY

E1 Regional similarities and differences

Regional differences and the concept of regionality lie at the heart of much recent discussion of the British Iron Age. Many studies have questioned the idea that a unified Iron Age actually existed, emphasising the often considerable differences which existed between different parts of Britain (and Ireland). These differences are seen not just as local variations on particular themes of material culture, but as characterising a wide range of ritual and social practices. While particularly evident in Britain and Ireland, they should not be seen as a peculiarity of these islands. Rather, Iron Age Europe as a whole was an Iron Age of regions.

Although regional differences have long been recognised, for example between the four provinces of the Scottish Iron Age (Piggott 1966), they are usually swamped by the notion that a single, uniform Iron Age existed, or explained mainly in terms of geographical and environmental factors. The belief that there was a single, coherent British Iron Age, with a distinct set of

Levels of preservation in the Western Isles machair: first century AD building with hearth at Cnip, Lewis (Photo: Historic Scotland, © Crown Copyright reserved)

common features (specific settlement types, objects, ritual practices and forms of social organisation) has been extremely strong over the last eighty years or more (cf Cunliffe 1991, 7–18). At the start of Iron Age studies, this approach was understandable given the need to extend typologies and interpretations from a small number of type-sites, usually in Wessex, to cover the whole of the country.

More recently, as more data have accumulated and underlying assumptions have been re-examined, the shortcomings of this approach have been exposed. In particular, we can now see that traditional models of the Iron Age are based very largely on features typical of limited areas of southern Britain (notably Wessex), which in turn have been used as a base line against which other parts of the island have been either explicitly or implicitly compared, often in a negative manner (cf Bevan 1999). The result of forcing the peculiarities of particular regions to fit a standard model and ignoring other differences, or even whole regions, which do not fit, has been to over-privilege Wessex and south-east England both in research, and in general accounts of the period. This focus also tends to reinforce the view that those parts of Britain closest to Europe were more highly developed than the 'peripheral' areas to the west and the north.

This view is increasingly difficult to sustain in the light of recent research across Britain, indicating consistent variations in settlement types, or mortuary and ritual practices, as well as different styles and uses of material culture. Some of the variations probably are a factor of climate and geography, but the term 'regionality' specifically describes characteristics that

Later Iron Age square enclosure at Blackhorse, Devon, excavated along the route of the A30 improvements in 1997 (Photo: W. Horner, © Devon County Council)

have to be explained in other ways. Differences between regions, such as those between East Yorkshire and its neighbours, or between north-east and Atlantic Scotland, point clearly to the construction and maintenance of distinct regional identities, often at varying scales. They also hint at different lifeways and social institutions in adjacent areas. As yet, these patterns are better known in some parts of Britain than others; characterising them properly is one of the key priorities facing Iron Age archaeology in the next decade.

The existence of marked regional differences in the way Iron Age societies were organised makes it harder to generalise from one part of Britain to another. Equally, the supposed centrality of events or processes in any one region can be questioned. All regions are important to reconstructing the complex social mosaic of the period, and need to be understood in their own right. There are, however, certain dangers in this new emphasis. Too much stress on regions could increase structural trends in British archaeology to focus narrowly on particular areas, leading to parochialism. For some phenomena, meaningful patterns only emerge through comparison with other regions, including those across the sea. Too narrow a focus could overlook supra-regional features of the British Iron Age that are manifested locally in different ways. These include living in round houses and selective adoption of particular aspects of the La Tène cultural 'package' by individual groups. Equally, there are underlying economic and social trends, such as later Iron Age settlement expansion (F2.2 below), which can be recognised across many different regions

There are considerable problems in tracing the regional mosaic of Iron Age Britain. The lack of a uniform level of knowledge throughout the island is the most important, a product both of academic interests over the last century, and more recently the uneven distribution of rescue excavations. Academic research has concentrated on a few 'key' regions like Atlantic Scotland, East Yorkshire and Wessex, all of which share highly visible surviving Iron Age monuments. In these regions, both the benefits and the dangers of letting research build on previous work are clear. Outside these regions, rescue archaeology has partly filled the gap, but this too has been concentrated in certain areas, particularly southern and eastern England. The lack of regional syntheses exacerbate the results of this uneven coverage (C2.1 above). More have been produced in recent years, especially in East Anglia (e.g. Davies 1996; Bryant 1997; Sealey 1996), but collation and presentation of the basic data is still a key priority for future work.

E2 Current state of regional knowledge

The rest of the section offers a subjective overview of existing knowledge about the Iron Age throughout England, Scotland and Wales, identifying those places where basic research is most needed (Table 3). Inevitably, there is a degree of artificiality in designating areas in this way, but this is unavoidable if we are to make comparisons covering the whole of Britain. We have not put forward priorities for individual areas, which is best done at the regional level (Olivier 1996). In the table, *Framework* denotes areas where regional frameworks and syntheses exist, or significant research is under-way; *Unsorted* indicates areas where some significant data are already collated in easily accessible form, but regional frameworks have not been developed, although *some* research to that end may be in progress; while the term *'Black hole'* is used colloquially for areas where site types are still ill-defined or unknown, and which have still seen relatively little modern research beyond the site-specific.

E2.1 Areas with established frameworks
As we have noted, areas with well established regional frameworks and syntheses are the exception, and they vary considerably in the degree of definition available.

In general, fieldwork in these areas should focus on clearly defined research themes, as well as exploiting any significant new opportunities which arise, for example through the discovery of unusual or well-preserved sites. With their abundant data sets, these are often the areas best suited to the evaluation of new theoretical interpretations through fieldwork or analysis of existing material; for example the study of spatial patterning in roundhouses in the Western Isles (Parker Pearson and Sharples 1999).

E2.2 Areas with partial frameworks
The areas classed as unsorted generally possess a fair amount of data relating to Iron Age settlement, often supported by material such as metalwork and coinage, for the most part well collated and accessible. Generally, however, there has been a failure to capital-ise on the results of previous surveys or research (for example, in south-east Perthshire; RCAHMS 1994), or to integrate the different categories of data. These areas would benefit particularly from longer-term research projects aimed at filling gaps in existing knowledge and are a prime target for regional synthesis. Without this, it is often difficult to assess how specific aspects of the Iron Age record compare to the most intensively studied regions.

E2.3 Areas without a framework
In the remaining areas such as Ayrshire, Derbyshire, Lancashire or the Welsh Valleys, archaeological understanding of the Iron Age has barely begun. Most have few known Iron Age sites, with little or no coherent history of investigation, and no easily accessible sources. In these areas, any discovery of Iron Age material has an importance of a different magnitude from other parts of Britain. Progress is likely to be through the identification of open or palisaded settlements, or from sampling enough undated sites of different forms to be able to predict which are potential Iron Age settlement types. That the situation can change relatively quickly as a result of new research, is shown by the case of the East Yorkshire lowlands (Halkon and Millett 1999) and the Mersey basin (Neville 1999), both of which would have figured in this category only a decade ago. The evidence of pollen analysis is also valuable in allowing the extent of human impact on the environment in the first millennium BC to be compared with regions where the settlement patterns are known in reasonable detail.

E3 Implementation

- regional variations are a central feature of the British Iron Age; defining and evaluating these differences should be a core objective of future research.

REGION	Framework	Unsorted	'Black hole'
Atlantic Scotland	Northern Isles, Western Isles	Caithness	Sutherland, West Highlands, Argyll, Ross and Cromarty
North-east Scotland		Perthshire, Angus·	Grampian, Stirling, Fife
South-east Scotland		East Lothian, Scottish Borders	Mid and West Lothian, Falkirk/ Clackmannan
South-west Scotland		Dumfries	Strathclyde, Galloway
North-east England	Northumberland, East Yorkshire	Durham; North, West and South Yorkshire	
North-west England			Cumbria, Lancashire
East Midlands		Lincolnshire, Leicestershire, Northamptonshire, Nottinghamshire, Bedfordshire	Derbyshire
West Midlands		Warwickshire, Herefordshire, Shropshire, Worcestershire	Cheshire, Birmingham
North Wales		Flintshire, Denbighshire, Anglesey and Gwynedd	Wrexham, Conwy
Mid Wales		Northern Powys	Central and Southern Powys
South Wales		Cardiff, Newport and coastal Monmouthshire, Swansea, Vale of Glamorgan	Welsh Valleys, Neath-Port Talbot and Bridgend, central and northern Monmouthshire
South-west Wales	Pembrokeshire and western Carmarthenshire		Cardiganshire and eastern Carmarthenshire
East Anglia	Hertfordshire, Essex, Norfolk	Suffolk, Cambridgeshire	
South-east England	Sussex	Kent, Greater London	Surrey
Southern-Central England	Upper Thames Valley, Central Wessex	Coastal Dorset, New Forest, Cotswolds and Mendips	West Dorset
South-west England	Cornwall, West Devon	Central Devon, Somerset	East Devon

Table 3. Existing knowledge of the Iron Age in different parts of Britain

- the substantial variations in current levels of knowledge between different parts of Britain seriously distort understanding of this period; efforts are needed to correct the balance and set better-known regions into proper context.
- in the blank areas, any opportunities for fieldwork on Iron Age sites should be treated as potentially significant for advancing under-standing at national level.
- many other areas would benefit from regional synthesis and from research projects aimed at filling gaps in the existing framework.

F. PROCESSES OF CHANGE

Although the apparent transformations in society in south-east England towards the end of the Iron Age have traditionally received particular attention, it is clear that other changes, just as deep, took place earlier in the period, and in other regions, even if the precise date and time scale is, in many cases, far from certain.

We will begin by examining developments in the centuries immediately following the widespread adoption of iron technology.

F1 Earlier pre-Roman Iron Age (c. 800 to 300 BC)

The transition from Bronze Age to Iron Age is now dated to the eighth century BC, the clearest archaeological indicator being the cessation of bronze hoarding, although this was not simultaneous across Britain (Taylor 1993). Despite the marked break in depositional practice, subsistence, settlement and pottery all show considerable continuities across the transition in most areas (e.g. Barrett 1980; Barrett *et al.* 1991) – although in Wales, pottery did apparently cease to be used altogether for a while in the earlier first millennium BC – so that a longer perspective, extending back into the second millennium BC, is essential to understanding both the adoption of iron and its various consequences

Cladh Hallan, South Uist, late Bronze Age/early Iron Age settlement mound: three roundhouses under excavation (© M. Parker Pearson)

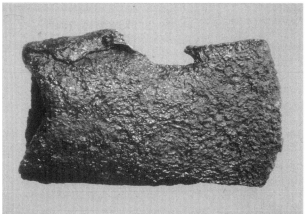

Iron socketed axe from Penllyn Moor, Vale of Cowbridge, South Glamorgan (© National Museum of Wales)

It should be stressed how little we know about social and economic developments in the first four or five centuries of the Iron Age in most of Britain. A great deal of our evidence relates to the later part of the period, from *c*. 300 BC onwards. The major excavation projects of the last 25 years have generally concerned later sites: even Danebury has relatively little evidence before the fifth century BC. This imbalance is itself a pointer to the differing character of earlier and later Iron Age settlements, the former often open and rather amorphous, the latter defined by banks and ditches, or multiple enclosures. The presence of enclosure is not however the only major difference. Other evidence – from the use of the landscape, to early Iron Age settlement distributions and pottery – hints at forms of social and territorial organisation different from the later period.

Whereas late Bronze Age, and to a lesser extent earlier Iron Age, metalwork is well documented, our knowledge of settlement and pottery sequences outside Wessex and the Thames Valley is relatively poor. In many regions, only a handful of settlements dating to this period have so far been identified or excavated (Haselgrove 1999b), although in certain others, the picture has been significantly modified as a result of a spate of new discoveries, as for instance, in the Severn

estuary (e.g. Whittle 1989; Nayling and Caseldine 1997). Thus it is hard to assess the character of much of Britain in the earlier first millennium BC, except through the nature and types of bronze and iron metalwork. In this context, any newly discovered late Bronze Age or earlier Iron Age site is potentially of greater importance than one of the later Iron Age.

F1.1 Metalworking

The end of bronze hoarding was a marked break in many areas, implying rapid social change. Despite local variation, Britain shares in the wider rhythms of deposition and stylistic change that typify the late Bronze and earlier Iron Ages of Western Europe (e.g. Cunliffe 1991; Champion 1999; Haselgrove 1999a). The basic metalwork typology is generally well established (although even now aspects of the chronology are open to revision; Needham *et al.* 1998), but much old material would benefit from re-examination, and the potential of metal-detector finds to illuminate regional patterns remains under-exploited (D1.1 above). The ritual or secular nature of bronze finds, and the mechanics of bronze exchange are still contentious, as is the articulation between metalwork use, social organisation and agriculture. Despite the smaller numbers of finds, similar questions need to be asked of early iron objects. More research is needed on the contexts of object use and deposition, both before and after the advent of iron (D2.2–D2.3 above).

When and why the transition to iron use occurred in different parts of Britain are key questions for future research. As yet, we have very little idea of the mechanisms of this process (D3.3.3 above). Iron was used to make some objects before the end of the Bronze Age and gradually becomes more common in the archaeological record between the eighth and third centuries BC (e.g. Salter and Ehrenreich 1984). There is however little close dating for early iron objects or working, while the recent redating of the end of the Ewart Park phase to *c*. 800 BC (Needham *et al.* 1998) merely emphasises the gap in our knowledge of how the industry developed. If the cessation of bronze hoarding and the adoption of iron for utilitarian objects are indeed related – as seems likely – this implies that iron was already common by the eighth century BC, but if so, the Llyn Fawr hoard (Savory 1976) and a limited number of iron socketed axes (Manning and Saunders 1972) are still virtually the only tangible evidence for the new technology. The context of early iron production and its relationship to bronze working is also poorly understood. To make progress in understanding the effects and time scale of this transition, one strategy would be to radiocarbon date metalworking residues – slags, moulds, crucibles and hearths `– from potentially early contexts. As noted above (D3.2.1), the role of flint technology at this period is another topic worthy of investigation (Ford *et al.* 1994).

F1.2 Settlement and agriculture

If the metalwork portrays a picture of marked change, this is not so with settlements and agriculture. Settlement forms and pottery styles show considerable continuity throughout the late Bronze Age and earlier Iron Age. Among other changes, the late Bronze Age saw increasing emphasis on elaborating the domestic sphere and on ritual deposition of agricultural produce, human remains and domestic objects (Champion 1999). These forms of ritual continued throughout the Iron Age.

The period up to 300 BC is characterised by an increasing variety of settlement forms across Britain. There is also increased evidence for the organisation and exploitation of the agricultural landscape, including linear boundaries, field systems, pit alignments and isolated wells and pits (e.g. Taylor 1997; Hill 1999). These features point to a dynamic pattern of agricultural intensification, with a number of innovations. Production of salt starts in the late Bronze Age and intensifies through the period (Bradley 1978), while there appears to be an increasing reliance on cereals in many areas, with spelt replacing emmer over much of eastern and southern Britain (Jones 1981; van der Veen 1992). The exact nature of regional farming systems is often poorly known, but complex patterns of local interdependence and transhumance are to be expected.

There were considerable differences within Britain. The best known regions, Wessex and the Thames Valley, may have only superficial similarities to other parts of the island (Hill 1995c). Large roundhouses are a feature of several areas at the time of the Bronze Age to Iron Age transition (e.g. Hingley 1995), although the apparent presence of long houses on some early first millennium BC sites should not be overlooked. Hillforts and other large enclosures were first constructed at this period in several areas of southern,

Early Iron Age pit alignment at the Cotswold Community site on the borders of Shorncote, Gloucestershire and Ashton Keynes, Wiltshire (© Oxford Archaeological Unit)

northern and western Britain, although the precise timing varies (Cunliffe 1991; Hill 1995c; Musson 1991; Needham and Ambers 1994), and the reasons for the marked increase in hillfort building remains an area of keen debate. Other regions lack hillforts altogether. In parts of eastern England, smaller heavily enclosed ringworks were occupied (Champion 1994). Midden sites such as East Chisenbury, Potterne and Runnymede in central-southern England should also be mentioned (McOmish 1996; Lawson 2000). Although not necessarily identical types of site, large, thick accumulations of cultural material dating to the early first millennium BC may be commoner than presumed.

It is important to recognise that other changes were taking place in this long period apart than those involving metalwork and hillfort construction. The social implications of 'the end of the Bronze Age' have only been discussed in fairly general terms, but even so have received decidedly more attention than social and economic changes in the earlier Iron Age. In part this is due to the lack of detailed chronologies to illuminate the degree of change and continuity in different regions. At present, late Bronze and early Iron Age

Pit burial in the unenclosed early Iron Age settlement at Battlesbury Bowl, Wiltshire, with Battlesbury hillfort in the background (© Wessex Archaeology)

pottery chronologies are only well defined in Wessex and the Thames Valley; elsewhere in southern England, broad changes in pottery styles are apparent, but more local refined sequences are needed. Hampering this is the lack of associations with dateable metalwork, and the problems of the calibration curve between 800 and 400 cal BC. Critical use of radiocarbon and other scientific dating methods, based on whatever materials are most appropriate, is essential for sites both with and without pottery (B2 above).

F2 Later pre-Roman Iron Age (c. 300 BC to AD 100)

The last four centuries of the Iron Age have received greater attention than the earlier period. This is due partly to the greater quantities of material of all kinds, and partly because of proximity to the Roman period. The significance of the later Iron Age as a starting point from which to measure the scale and nature of change following the Roman conquest has rightly been given prominence: the original *Exploring our Past* (English Heritage 1991, 36) singled out 'Briton into Roman *c.* 300 BC–AD 200' as a central theme for research and

excavation. We must, nevertheless, recognise the dangers of analysing indigenous developments primarily from the perspective of social and economic changes after the Roman conquest; other, equally important transformations may be completely overlooked. Specific questions need to be asked of the later Iron Age, rather than its being subsumed into separate issues concerning the transition to Roman rule, a point which is recognised in the revised edition of *Exploring our Past* (English Heritage 1998a).

Traditionally the period has been divided into the middle and late Iron Age, the latter being distinguished by new forms of material culture such as coins and wheel made pottery, as well as new settlement types and ritual practices (cf Cunliffe 1991; 1995b). Many of these changes are, however, confined to certain parts of southern and eastern England. In other areas, such as East Sussex, Norfolk and the Fenlands, the 'middle Iron Age' – as defined by its pottery – continues up to the Roman conquest and beyond (Haselgrove 1987, 58–63; Hill 1999). Moreover, many 'late Iron Age' developments can now be seen either to have started earlier, or to be rooted in developments prior to 100 BC (Haselgrove 1989). They cannot be understood purely in terms of external causes in the first century BC. It is thus increasingly hard to sustain the traditional separation between a 'middle' and 'late' Iron Age even in southern Britain, let alone the island as a whole (Hill 1995c). Rather, the traits that typify parts of southern and eastern England in the first centuries BC and AD are another example of the regionality which typifies Iron Age Britain. In their turn, these features can be seen as part of a broader pattern of change which began *c.* 400–200 BC and intensified in many regions towards the end of the millennium.

F2.1 The earlier to later Iron Age transition
Viewed as a whole, there are significant differences between Britain in *c.* 500 BC and Britain in *c.* 50 BC. It is not simply that the evidence is more abundant; recent work is also suggesting substantive differences in the range and forms of social processes at work. These differences are poorly understood, partly because they are only now being recognised, and partly because they represent the outcome of a gradual transformation over several centuries. The dating of this earlier to later Iron Age transition is only securely known in Wessex, and the adoption of 'middle Iron Age' pottery need not have taken place simultaneously everywhere (B1 above). Neither the causes of this change in ceramic styles, nor the nature of broader social changes between *c.* 500 to 300 BC have so far been investigated in any detail. In all areas, there is need for more radiocarbon dating, as well as additional associations between pottery and other dateable objects (B2.1–2.5 above).

One of the most striking features of the later Iron Age is the sheer abundance of evidence of different

Silver coin of Tincomaros, late first century BC (© Celtic Coin Index, Oxford)

Haddenham, Cambridgeshire: excavated roundhouse and enclosure ditch (Photo: C. Evans, © Cambridge Archaeological Unit)

kinds, whether numbers of settlements or the quantities of material culture found on them, as well as in burials, on religious sites, and in a variety of 'off-site' locations. Although this material provides plentiful data for research, only rarely are the reasons behind this abundance questioned (Hill 1997). Equally, while regional variations in material culture and social practice are particularly visible in the period after 300 BC, we need to establish how much this is due to the greater quantity and variety of evidence, how much to a genuine intensification of regional differences at this time. By the first century BC, however, the distinctions in material culture, ritual, and settlement types across Britain do seem sufficiently clear cut to imply real differences in social organisation between regions.

F2.2 Settlement expansion

Another feature of the later Iron Age is settlement expansion and ever intensifying use of the landscape, almost certainly linked to a significant rise in population (Haselgrove 1984; 1989; Hill 1995c). The closing centuries of the first millennium BC saw settlement expansion into many previously sparsely settled areas and wetland regions like the Fens of eastern England or the Avon Levels in the Severn Estuary (e.g. at Hallen; Gardiner *et al.* forthcoming), and the infilling of others, so that by the first century AD, large parts of the lowland landscape were virtually 'full' of settlement (Hill 1999). It seems likely that prior to this period, many areas were relatively sparsely occupied and exploited; one reason being that the fertile but heavy soils which characterise many of the relevant areas were previously probably relatively difficult to cultivate. The use of iron-tipped plough shares and cereal crops suited to heavier soils and the introduction of the rotary quern, together with the climatic improvements after 400 BC, undoubtedly assisted the expansion (Haselgrove 1984, 17–19), although as some writers have noted (e.g. Hill 1995b; Tipping 1997), the impetus to agricultural expansion may have come from changes in social organisation.

This expansion into thinly-settled areas and the social processes underlying this phenomenon are increasingly emerging as one of the crucial features of the later Iron Age (Hill 1999). Frequently, the expansion process is linked with developing craft specialisation and production for non-local exchange (Haselgrove 1989), for instance in the working of iron, pottery and glass, as well as with new kinds of settlement, which might in turn indicate new forms of social organisation. In some cases, the colonisation of new land was apparently accompanied by the laying out of extensive field systems as in East Anglia and the North Midlands (e.g. Williamson 1987; Chadwick 1999) – although better dating evidence is needed – while in others, settlement expansion may have promoted agricultural innovation. One notable exception to the prevailing trend is Wessex, where the heyday of developed hillforts like Danebury and Maiden Castle seems to co-incide with the virtual depopulation of their immediate environs (Sharples 1991b; Cunliffe 2000). The pattern in the Welsh Marches, the northern part of the same hillfort-dominated zone, may well be different, again underlining the relevance of regional context. All these phenomena require further investigation, both to understand the mechanisms at work locally, and to assess to what extent similar processes were operating throughout different regions of both lowland and upland Britain.

F2.3 Southern and eastern England

It is into this context that developments after *c.* 150 BC in southern and eastern England - such as the adoption of coinage, visible burial rites and shrines; revitalised exchange links; and the emergence of new large-scale settlements (*oppida*) – must be set. The transition from middle to late Iron Age in southern Britain was once characterised as a seamless passage from hillforts to *oppida*, driven to a large extent by increasing trade with the continent. Changes in south-east England were a peripheral product of changes on the continent, brought about by the expansion of Rome, while other parts of Britain were in turn peripheral to the South-East (Haselgrove 1982; Cunliffe 1991). This simple

Silchester, Hampshire: timber building on the alignment of the Iron Age street in Insula IX (Photo: A. Clark, © University of Reading)

Stanwick, North Yorkshire: monumental circular structure in the Tofts, mid first century AD (© C. Haselgrove)

model has, however, come under sustained critique over the last fifteen years and developing more sophisticated alternatives is a priority for future synthesis and excavation. In the third century BC, southern Britain saw the re-emergence of gold, absent since the late Bronze Age, although it did not start to be deposited in the ground in any quantity before the mid second century BC. Torcs and coins were clearly among the media used to articulate social relations (Haselgrove 1987), and their appearance could have had a disruptive effect upon existing systems. Parts of southern Britain also show an increase in the use of horse trappings at about the same period. As yet the relationship between the various changes are poorly understood – work at sites like Danebury, Hengistbury, Maiden Castle and Westhampnett having raised as nearly as many questions as they answered.

Chronologies, artefact assemblages and sites are better known from the later first century BC onward. Rapid changes took place, with the foundation of *oppida* like Colchester, Silchester and St Albans, and intensified contacts with Gaul and the Mediterranean world. Many of the principal oppida were established in areas where earlier settlement was sparse (Hill 1995c; 1999), indicating the need to consider their emergence in relation to processes of settlement expansion in other parts of Britain. There were notable changes in the forms, imagery and distribution of coinage (Creighton 2000), as well as significant alterations in personal appearance, ways of eating, and in the nature of domestic architecture. These transformations are associated with the development of 'kingdoms' – large scale polities with clear signs of social hierarchy and elites – and are essentially confined to south-east England. Explaining them remains a key challenge. Here, the scale and nature of contacts with the Roman world, and with the imperial aristocracy in particular, is an area for considerable debate.

The next few years should see publication of further major excavations directly relevant to these issues (e.g. Hayling Island temple, Heybridge 'small town'). Nevertheless, major lacunae exist even for this relatively well known period. Despite the recent work at Silchester and St Albans (Fulford and Timby 2000; Niblett 1999), *oppida* in general remain poorly understood and evidence for spheres such as agricultural and craft production, rural settlements, and territorial organisation is limited. Even in the heartlands of the two major kingdoms north and south of the Thames, the adoption of new practices, artefact types and social forms seems to be both selective and variable in date (Hill forthcoming), while in adjacent regions, the chronology of wheel-turned pottery and other late Iron Age forms is poorly known. Outside south-east England, the new burial traditions and ritual sites which emerge in this period have received little recent attention. In East Anglia and Lincolnshire, for example, the quantity of metalwork and coinage recovered from many probable settlement sites implies cult activity there (Willis 1997), but none of them have as yet been excavated on a large scale. There are also signs that some of the larger aggregations which typify certain parts of eastern England are actually a product of fluid, shifting settlement patterns, similar to those found in other regions bordering the North Sea (Hill 1999), rather than representing stable nucleated villages. This would have important implications for the social organisation of the communities in question and requires further work.

F2.4 Northern and western England, Scotland and Wales

Elsewhere in Britain, the paucity of well-understood regional sequences, longevity of material culture forms and lack of pottery, present major obstacles to the investigation of the nature and timing of changes at the end of the Iron Age and into the period of Roman domination. Despite the opaque character of the material culture, it is likely that there were some moves towards political centralisation and greater social complexity (e.g. Foster 1989; Armit 1999). Here again, routine use of absolute dating is essential for progress. In some areas, enclosed sites – having multiplied during the final centuries BC – appear to have given way to more open forms of settlement before the Roman occupation, although we should not overlook the probability that in many areas open sites also formed a significant component of settlement patterns dominated by the more easily detected enclosures (e.g. Haselgrove 1984; 1999).

As in parts of southern and eastern England, there are indications of greater emphasis on the individual at the expense of the community, such as larger numbers of personal ornaments or the use of formal burial. The conspicuous consumption of wealth through deposition of metalwork and other goods also increases in many areas at this time. Not all regions show such changes, however, a reminder of the difficulty of generalising across Britain at any stage of the Iron Age. The impact of the Roman occupation on Iron Age settlement forms and the often highly selective uptake of Romanised material culture both within and beyond the frontier remain key areas for further research.

F3 Implementation

F3.1 Earlier pre-Roman Iron Age
- the earlier Iron Age is particularly poorly understood. In the present state of knowledge, all sites of this period, however ephemeral, have a high research priority.
- excavation of a range of late Bronze Age/earlier Iron Age settlement types and landscape features is needed in all areas.
- chronology is a major problem for the earlier first millennium BC. Research is needed on regional pottery sequences, supported by absolute dating programmes.
- investigation of the contexts of late Bronze Age and early Iron Age metalwork is vital to understand the changing roles of these objects. This includes the excavation of discovery sites, but also consideration of their wider landscape setting.
- the organisation, location and scale of early iron production and its relationship to other technologies (including flint) are poorly understood. It is essential that finds of early metalworking residues are well dated.

F3.2 Later pre-Roman Iron Age
- more precise chronologies are required to understand the rate, scale and cause of economic and social changes during the later

Aerial view of excavation and reconstructed Iron Age village at Castell Henllys, Pembrokeshire (© Pembrokeshire Coast National Park Authority)

Iron Age. Routine use of absolute dating techniques is essential.
- the nature of the archaeological transition between the earlier and later Iron Age (c. 500 to 300 BC) requires particular attention.
- the increased abundance of material on many later Iron Age sites needs quantification and explanation.
- the cause and consequences of settlement expansion in different parts of Britain after c. 300 BC requires further research.
- contemporary changes in the organisation, intensity and scale of agricultural and craft production require detailed local investigation and inter-regional comparison.
- new models need to be developed to explain the archaeological changes in southern and eastern England during the last two centuries of the period.
- more research is needed into the nature and degree of social and political changes in parts of Britain outside the south-east .

G. CONCLUSION

The paper has examined five broad areas which are central to future research on the British Iron Age. In each case, we have sought to identify specific topics on which work is imperative or could fruitfully be encouraged, based on our current understanding of the period and deficiencies in the known record. We have also highlighted certain areas where changes in archaeological practice would be beneficial. Inevitably, some themes run from one section to another, such as the need for routine radiocarbon dating and integrated, contextual analysis of all types of data in a wider landscape setting. As we noted in the introduction, a key aim of this review is to provide support for local curatorial decisions, while ensuring that research opportunities brought about by developer-funding are realised to the full. At the same time, we believe that the general framework that the paper provides will be of value in helping to shape more detailed research agendas formulated at regional level and in articulating these with research issues at national level. The priorities set out here must not however be viewed as immutable, nor do they claim to be comprehensive; rather it is up to the community as a whole to ensure that they are continually evolved as existing problems are resolved, and new questions and approaches come to the fore.

H. APPENDIX: PUBLICATIONS ON IRON AGE BRITAIN, 1990–1999

As part of the study, an analysis of published output on Iron Age sites and topics since 1990 was conducted using the information contained in *British* (now *and Irish*) *Archaeological Abstracts*. The results are set out in Table 4. Although the figures show considerable variation across the categories, they reveal a pattern that has remained remarkably constant for a decade.

The publication figures seem intuitively to be a fair reflection of activity over the period. The overwhelming dominance of settlement studies (category G) reflects the growth of developer-funded archaeology, where the nature of evaluations encourages reporting of sites found. The relatively high numbers in categories H and K reflect recent academic interest in topics such as structured deposition, hillforts and brochs. Category F (artefacts) may seem large, but many of the items are reports on single objects rather than larger-scale studies. The comparatively low numbers in category D, especially regional surveys, reflects the comparative lack of attempts to synthesise the rapidly growing mass of detailed evidence (C2.1 above).

Year	A	B	C	D	E	F	G	H	J	K
1990	1	3	6	5	12	8	38	11	-	-
1991	0	6	5	5	5	5	20	5	-	-
1992	1	8	4	4	6	11	17	10	0	21
1993	2	4	2	1	4	9	20	6	0	6
1994	0	11	4	2	3	9	22	5	0	7
1995	0	1	0	2	4	1	17	2	1	2
1996	2	5	2	1	3	12	15	5	1	10
1997	1	4	9	2	5	12	22	5	0	12
1998	2	5	1	2	5	5	29	13	1	5
1999	0	4	6	5	6	8	20	9	0	8
Total	9	51	39	29	53	80	220	71	3	71

A: Principles, history, bibliography, museology, conservation
B: Fieldwork, recording, analysis, environmental, experimental
C: Texts, coins, inscriptions
D: Cultural, political and historical surveys
E: Communications, technology, trade, agriculture
F: Artefacts
G: Settlement
H: Funerary and cult
J: Secular architecture
K: Warfare and defence

Table 4. Publications on the Iron Age included in British *(now and Irish)* Archaeological Abstracts *from 1990*

I. Bibliography

Allason-Jones, L and Jones, D M 1994. Jet and other materials in Roman artefact studies, *Archaeol Aeliana* (Ser 5) 22, 265–272.

Andrews, G and Barrett, J 1997. *Research Design for the Heathrow Terminal 5 Project.*

Armit, I 1989. Broch building in northern Scotland: the context of innovation, *World Archaeol* 21, 435–445.

Armit, I 1991. The Atlantic Scottish Iron Age: five levels of chronology, *Proc Soc Antiq Scot* 121, 181–214.

Armit, I 1996. *The Archaeology of Skye and the Western Isles.* Edinburgh: Univ Press.

Armit, I 1997. *Celtic Scotland.* Edinburgh: Historic Scotland.

Armit, I 1999. Life after Hownam: the Iron Age in south–east Scotland, in Bevan (ed) 1999, 65–80.

Armit, I, Dunwell, A J and Hunter, F 1999. Traprain Law, *Discovery and Excavation in Scotland* 1999, 30–31.

Armit, I, Dunwell, A J and Hunter, F 2000. Traprain Law, *Discovery and Excavation in Scotland* 2000, 29.

Armit, I, Dunwell, A J and Campbell, E forthcoming. *Excavation of an Iron Age, Early Historic and Medieval Settlement and Metal-working Site at Eilean Olabhat, North Uist.*

Ashmore, P J 1999. Radiocarbon dating: avoiding errors by avoiding mixed samples, *Antiquity* 73, 124–130.

Barber, J W and Crone, B A 1993. Crannogs. a diminishing resource? A survey of the crannogs of south-west Scotland and excavations at Buiston Crannog, *Antiquity* 67, 520–533.

Barclay, G J (ed) 1997. *State-funded 'Rescue' Archaeology in Scotland. Past, Present and Future.* Edinburgh: Hist Scotl Anc Monum Division Occ Pap 2.

Barker, G W and Gamble, C S (eds) 1985. *Beyond Domestication in Prehistoric Europe.* London: Academic Press.

Barnett, S M 2000. Luminescence dating of pottery from later prehistoric Britain, *Archaeometry* 42, 431–457.

Barrett, J C 1980. The pottery of the later Bronze Age in lowland England, *Proc Prehist Soc* 46, 297–320.

Barrett, J C 1989. Food, gender and metal: questions of social reproduction, in M L Sørensen and R Thomas (eds), *The Bronze Age–Iron Age Transition in Europe*, 304–320. Oxford: BAR S483.

Barrett, J C, Bradley, R, and Green, M 1991. *Landscape, Monuments and Society. The Prehistory of Cranborne Chase.* Cambridge: Univ Press.

Barrett, J, Freeman, P and Woodward, A 2000. *Cadbury Castle, Somerset: the later prehistoric and early historic archaeology.* London: English Heritage Archaeol Rep 20.

Bateson, J D and Holmes, N M McQ, 1997. Roman and medieval coins found in Scotland, 1988–95, *Proc Soc Antiq Scot* 127, 527–561.

Bayley, J 1990. The production of brass in antiquity with particular reference to Roman Britain, in Craddock (ed), *2000 Years of Zinc and Brass*, 7–27. London: Brit Mus.

Bayley, J 1992. *Non-Ferrous Metalworking from Coppergate.* York: CBA and York Archaeol Trust.

Bayley, J 1998. Metals and metalworking in the first millennium AD, in Bayley (ed) 1998, 161–168.

Bayley, J (ed) 1998. *Science in Archaeology: an Agenda for the Future.* London: English Heritage.

Bayley, J and Butcher, S 1981. Variations in alloy composition of Roman brooches, *Revue d'Archéometrie, Supplément*, 29–36.

Bayliss, A 1998. Some thoughts on using scientific dating in English archaeology and building analysis for the next decade, in Bayley (ed) 1998, 95–108.

Bayliss, A, Groves, C, McCormack, G, Baillie, M, Brown, D and Brennand, M 1999. Precise dating of the Norfolk timber circle, *Nature* 402, 479.

Bell, M 1996. Environment in the first millennium BC, in Champion and Collis (eds) 1996, 5–16.

Bell, M, Caseldine, A, and Neumann, H 2000. *Prehistoric Intertidal Archaeologiy in the Welsh Severn Estuary.* York: CBA Res Rep 120.

Bender Jørgensen, L 1992. *North European Textiles until AD 1000.* Aarhus: Univ Press.

Bevan, B 1997. Bounding the landscape: place and identity during the Yorkshire Wolds Iron Age, in Gwilt and Haselgrove (eds) 1997, 181–191.

Bevan, B (ed) 1999. *Northern Exposure: interpretative devolution and the Iron Ages in Britain.* Leicester: Leicester Archaeol Monogr 4.

Bewley, R H 1994. *Prehistoric and Romano-British Settlement on the Solway Plain, Cumbria.* Oxford: Oxbow Monogr 17.

Biggins, J A, Biggins, J, Coxon, R and Watson, M 1997. Survey of the prehistoric settlement at Gardener's Houses Farm, Dinnington, *Durham Archaeol J* 13, 43–54.

Bishop, M C 1988. Cavalry equipment of the Roman army in the first century AD, in J C Coulston (ed), *Military Equipment and the Identity of Roman Soldiers*, 67–195. Oxford: BAR S394.

Bishop, M C and Coulston, J N C 1993. *Roman Military Equipment.* London.

Bonnamour, L and Dumont, A 1996. Les armes romaines de la Saône: état des découvertes et données récentes de fouilles, in C van Driel-Murray (ed), *Military Equipment in Context (J Roman Military Equipment Studies* 5), 141–154.

Bowden, M and McOmish, D 1987 The required barrier, *Scottish Archaeol Rev* 4, 76–84.

Bradley, R 1978. *The Prehistoric Settlement of Britain.* London: Routledge & Keegan Paul.

Bradley, R 1990. *The Passage of Arms*. Cambridge: Univ Press.

Bradley, R, Entwhistle, R, and Raymond, F 1994. *Prehistoric Land Divisions on Salisbury Plain*. London: English Heritage.

Brewster, T C M 1963. *The Excavation of Staple Howe*. Scarborough: East Riding Archaeological Research Committee.

Brown, L 1997 Marketing and commerce in late Iron Age Dorset: the Wareham/Poole harbour pottery industry, in Gwilt and Haselgrove (eds) 1997, 40–46.

Bryant, S 1997. Iron Age, in Glazebrook (ed) 1997, 23–34.

Budd, P and Taylor, T, 1995. The faerie smith meets the bronze industry: magic versus science in the interpretation of prehistoric metal-making, *World Archaeol* 27, 133–143.

Campbell, E, 1991. Excavations of a wheelhouse and other Iron Age structures at Sollas, North Uist, by R J C Atkinson in 1957, *Proc Soc Antiq Scot* 121, 117–173.

CBA 1948. *A Survey and Policy of Field Research in the Archaeology of Great Britain I: Prehistoric and Early Historic Ages to the Seventh Century AD*. London: CBA.

Chadwick, A 1999. Digging ditches but missing riches? Ways into the Iron Age and Romano-British cropmark landscapes of the north Midlands, in Bevan (ed) 1999, 149–172.

Champion, T C 1994. Socio-economic development in eastern England in the first millennium BC, in K Kristiansen and J Jensen (eds), *Europe in the First Millennium BC*, 125–144. Sheffield: Sheffield Archaeol Monogr 6.

Champion, T C 1999. The later Bronze Age, in Hunter and Ralston (eds) 1999, 95–112.

Champion, T C and Collis, J R (eds) 1996. *The Iron Age in Britain and Ireland: recent trends*. Sheffield: J R Collis.

Cheape, H 1988. Food and liquid containers in the Hebrides: a window on the Iron Age, in Fenton and Myrdal (eds), *Food and Drink and Travelling Accessories*, 6–27. Edinburgh: John Donald.

Clark, G 1951. Folk-culture and the study of European prehistory, in W F Grimes (ed), *Aspects of Archaeology in Britain and Beyond*, 49–65. London: Edwards.

Clarke, D L 1972. A provisional model of an Iron Age society and its settlement system, in D L Clarke (ed), *Models in Archaeology*, 801–869. London: Methuen.

Clarke, D V 1971. Small finds in the Atlantic province: problems of approach, *Scottish Archaeol Forum* 3, 22–54.

Clogg P W and Ferrell G 1991. Geochemical survey in Northumberland, *Northern Archaeol* 11, 43–50.

Coles, J and Minnitt, S 1995. 'Industrious and fairly civilized': the Glastonbury Lake Village. Taunton: Somerset Levels Project, Somerset County Council.

Collis, J R 1994. The Iron Age, in B Vyner (ed), *Building on the Past: papers celebrating 150 years of the Royal Archaeological Institute*, 123–148.

Cool, H E M 1982. The artefact record: some possibilities, in Harding (ed) 1982, 92–100.

Cool, H E M, Lloyd-Morgan, G and Hooley, A D 1995. *Finds from the Fortress*. York: CBA and York Archaeol Trust.

Cowell, M 1992. An analytical survey of the British Celtic gold coinage, in Mays (ed) 1992, 207–233.

Craig, O, Mulville, J, Parker Pearson, M, Sokol, R, Gelsthorpe, K, Stacey, R, and Collins, M 2000. Detecting milk proteins in ancient pots, *Nature* 408, 312.

Creighton, J 2000. *Coins and Power in Late Iron Age Britain*. Cambridge: Univ Press.

Crew, P 1991. The experimental production of prehistoric bar iron, *Hist Metall* 25, 21–36.

Crew, P 1995 Aspects of the iron supply, in Cunliffe 1995a, 276–284.

Crummy, N 1983. *The Roman Small Finds from Excavations in Colchester 1971–9*. Colchester: Colchester Archaeol Trust Archaeol Rep 2.

Cunliffe, B W 1984. *Danebury: An Iron Age Hillfort in Hampshire. Vol 2. The Excavations 1969–78: the finds*. London: CBA Res Rep 52.

Cunliffe, B W 1991. *Iron Age Communities in Britain*. London: Routledge.

Cunliffe, B W 1992. Pits, preconceptions and propitiation in the British Iron Age, *Oxford J Archaeol* 11, 69–84.

Cunliffe, B W 1995a. *Danebury: an Iron Age Hillfort in Hampshire. Vol 6. A Hillfort Community in Perspective*. York: CBA Res Rep 102.

Cunliffe, B W 1995b. *Iron Age Britain*. London: English Heritage.

Cunliffe, B W 1996. The Celtic chariot: a footnote, in Raftery (ed) 1996, 31–39.

Cunliffe, B W 2000. *The Danebury Environs Programme: the prehistory of a Wessex landscape. Vol. 1 Introduction*. Oxford: English Heritage and OUCA Monogr 48.

Cunliffe, B W and Poole, C 1991. *Danebury: An Iron Age Hillfort in Hampshire. Vol 4. The Excavations 1969–78: the site*. London: CBA Res Rep 73.

Cunliffe, B W and Poole, C 2000. *The Danebury Environs Programme: the Prehistory of a Wessex Landscape Vol. 2, Parts 1–7*. Oxford: English Heritage and OUCA Monogr 49.

Cunliffe, B W and Miles, D (eds) 1984. *Aspects of the Iron Age in Central Southern Britain*. Oxford: OUCA Monogr 2.

Curteis, M 1996. An analysis of the circulation patterns of Iron Age coins from Northamptonshire, *Britannia* 27, 17–42.

Davies, J 1996. Where Eagles dare: the Iron Age of Norfolk, *Proc Prehist Soc* 62, 63–92.

Dent, J S 1982. Cemeteries and settlement patterns of the Iron Age on the Yorkshire Wolds, *Proc Prehist Soc* 48, 437–457.

Dent, J 1983. Weapons, wounding and war in the Iron Age, *Archaeol J* 140, 120–128.

DCMS 1999. *Portable Antiquities: Annual Report 1997–98*. London: Dept Culture, Media and Sport.

DCMS 2000. *Portable Antiquities: Annual Report 1998–99*. London: Dept Culture, Media and Sport.

DCMS 2001. *Portable Antiquities: Annual Report 1999–2000*. London: Dept Culture, Media and Sport.

Dobinson, C and Denison, S 1995. *Metal Detecting and Archaeology in England*. London: CBA/English Heritage.

Drewett, P 1982. Later Bronze Age downland economy and excavation at Black Patch, East Sussex, *Proc Prehist Soc* 48, 321–400.

Dudd, N and Evershed, R 1998. Direct demonstration of milk as an element of archaeological economies, *Science* 282, 1478–1481.

Dungworth, D B 1996. The production of copper alloys in Iron Age Britain, *Proc Prehist Soc* 62, 399–421.

Dungworth, D B 1997. Roman copper alloys: analysis of artefacts from Northern Britain, *J Archaeol Sci* 24, 901–910

Dunning, G C 1934. The swan's-neck and ring-headed pin of the British Iron Age, *Archaeol J* 91, 269–295.

Dunwell, A J and Strachan, R forthcoming. *Excavations at the Brown and White Caterthuns, Angus*.

Earwood, C 1991. Two Early Historic bog butter containers, *Proc Soc Antiq Scot* 121, 231–240.

Earwood, C 1993. *Domestic Wooden Artefacts in Britain and Ireland from Neolithic to Viking Times*. Exeter: Univ Exeter Press.

Ehrenreich, R M 1991. Metalworking in Iron Age Britain: hierarchy or heterarchy?, in R M Ehrenreich (ed), *Metals in Society: theory beyond regional analysis*, 69–80. Philadelphia: MASCA.

Ehrenreich, R M 1994. Ironworking in Iron Age Wessex, in Fitzpatrick and Morris (eds) 1994, 16–18.

English Heritage 1991. *Exploring our Past*. London: English Heritage.

English Heritage 1998a. *Exploring our Past 1998*. London: English Heritage.

English Heritage 1998b. *Implementation plan for Exploring our Past 1998*. London: English Heritage.

Eogan, G 1983. Ribbon torcs in Britain and Ireland, in B O'Connor and D V Clarke (eds), *From the Stone Age to the 'Forty-Five'*, 87–126. Edinburgh: John Donald.

Evans, C 1989. Perishables and worldly goods – artifact decoration and classification in the light of wetlands research, *Oxford J Archaeol* 8, 179–201.

Evans, J 1995. Later Iron Age and 'native' pottery in the north-east, in B Vyner (ed), *Moorland Monuments: studies in the archaeology of north-east Yorkshire in honour of Raymond Hayes and Donald Spratt*, 46–68. York: CBA Res Rep 101.

Fasham, P 1985. *The Prehistoric Settlement at Winnall Down, Winchester*. Winchester: Hampshire Field Club Monograph 2.

Fell, V 1997. Iron Age iron files from England, *Oxford J Archaeol* 16, 79–98.

Fell, V 1998. Iron Age ferrous hammerheads from Britain, *Oxford J Archaeol* 17, 207–225.

Fenton, A 1978. *The Northern Isles: Orkney and Shetland*. Edinburgh: John Donald.

Ferrell, G 1997. Space and society in the Iron Age of north-east England, in Gwilt and Haselgrove (eds) 1997, 228–238.

Field, N and Parker Pearson, M forthcoming. *Fiskerton: an Iron Age timber causeway with Iron Age and Roman votive offerings*. Oxford: Oxbow.

Fitts, R L, Haselgrove, C C, Lowther, P C and Willis, S H 1999. Melsonby revisited: survey and excavation 1992–95 at the site of the discovery of the "Stanwick", North Yorkshire, hoard of 1843, *Durham Archaeol J* 14, 1–52.

Fitzpatrick, A P 1984. The deposition of La Tène Iron Age metalwork in watery contexts in southern England, in Cunliffe and Miles (eds) 1984, 178–190.

Fitzpatrick, A P 1991. Celtic (Iron Age) religion – traditional and timeless? *Scott Archaeol Rev* 8, 123–129

Fitzpatrick, A P 1997a. *Archaeological Excavations on the Route of the A27 Westhampnett Bypass, West Sussex: Volume 2: the cemeteries*. Salisbury: Wessex Archaeol Rep 12.

Fitzpatrick, A P 1997b. Everyday life in Iron Age Wessex, in Gwilt and Haselgrove (eds) 1997, 73–86.

Fitzpatrick, A P and Morris, E (eds) 1994. *The Iron Age in Wessex: recent work*. Salisbury: Association Française D'Etude de L'Age du Fer/Trust for Wessex Archaeology.

Fitzpatrick, A P, Barnes, I and Cleal, R M J 1995. An Early Iron Age settlement at Dunston Park, Thatcham, in I Barnes *et al.*, *Early Settlement in Berkshire: Mesolithic – Roman occupation sites in the Thames and Kennet Valleys*, 65–92. Salisbury: Wessex Archaeol Rep 6.

Ford, S, Bradley, R, Hawkes, J, and Fisher, P 1984. Flint-working in the metal age, *Oxford J Archaeol* 3, 157–174.

Foster, J 1980. *The Iron Age Moulds from Gussage All Saints*. London: Brit Mus Occas Pap 12.

Foster, J 1996. Metalworking in the British Iron Age: the evidence from Weelsby Avenue, Grimsby, in Raftery (eds) 1996, 49–61.

Foster, S 1989. Analysis of spatial patterns in buildings (gamma analysis) as an insight into social structure: Examples from the Scottish Atlantic Iron Age, *Antiquity* 63, 40–50.

Fox., C F 1958. *Pattern and Purpose: a survey of Early Celtic Art in Britain*. Cardiff.

Foxon, A 1991. *Bone, Antler, Tooth and Horn Technology and Utilisation in Prehistoric Scotland*. Unpubl PhD thesis, Univ Glasgow.

Fulford, M and Timby, J 2000. *Late Iron Age and Roman Silchester: excavations on the site of the forum-basilica 1977, 1980–86*. London: Britannia Monogr 15.

Gardiner, J 1993. The flint assemblage, in J A Davies, Excavation of an Iron Age pit group at London Road, Thetford, *Norfolk Archaeol* 41, 456–8.

Gardiner, J, Allen, M J, Hamilton-Dyer, S, Laidlaw, M, and Scaife, R, forthcoming. Making the most of it: later prehistoric pastoralism in the Avon Levels, Severn Estuary, *Proc Prehist Soc* 68.

Giles, M 2000. *Close-knit, Open-weave: archaeologies of identity in the later prehistoric landscape of East Yorkshire*. Unpubl PhD thesis, Univ Sheffield.

Gillings, M and Pollard, J 1999. Non-portable stone artefacts and the contexts of meaning: the tale of Grey Wether, *World Archaeol* 31, 179–193.

Glazebrook, J (ed) 1997. *Research and Archaeology: a framework for the Eastern Counties*. Norwich: E Anglian Archaeol Occas Pap 3.

Grant, A 1984a. Animal husbandry, in Cunliffe 1984, 496–546.

Grant, A 1984b. Animal husbandry in Wessex and the Thames Valley, in Cunliffe and Miles (eds) 1984, 102–119.

Guido, M 1978. *The Glass Beads of the Prehistoric and Roman Periods in Britain and Ireland*. London: Rep Res Comm Soc Antiq London 35.

Gwilt, A 1997. Popular practices from material culture: a case study of the Iron Age settlement at Wakerley, Northamptonshire, in Gwilt and Haselgrove (eds) 1997, 153–166.

Gwilt, A and Haselgrove, C C (eds) 1997. *Reconstructing Iron Age Societies*. Oxford: Oxbow Monogr 71.

Halkon, P 1997. Fieldwork on early iron working sites in East Yorkshire, *Hist Metall* 31, 12–16.

Halkon, P. and Millett. M. (eds) 1999. Rural settlement and industry: studies in the Iron Age and Roman archaeology of lowland East Yorkshire. Leeds: *Yorks Archaeol Rep* 4.

Hallén, Y 1994. The use of bone and antler at Foshigarry and Bac Mhic Connain, two Iron Age sites on North Uist, Western Isles, *Proc Soc Antiq Scot* 124, 189–231.

Hambleton, E 1999. *Animal Husbandry Regimes in Iron Age Britain: a comparative analysis of faunal assemblages from British Iron Age sites*. Oxford: BAR 282.

Harding, D W (ed) 1982. *Later Prehistoric Settlement in South-east Scotland*, Univ Edinburgh: Dept Archaeol Occas Pap 8.

Harrison, D 1992. The Celtic Coin Index, in Mays (ed) 1992, xv–xvi

Hartley, M and Ingilby, J 1990. *Life and Tradition in the Moorlands of North-east Yorkshire*. Otley: Smith Settle.

Hartley, M and Ingilby, J 1997. *Life and Tradition in the Yorkshire Dales*. Otley: Smith Settle.

Haselgrove, C C 1982. Wealth, prestige and power: the dynamics of late Iron Age centralisation in south eastern England, in C Renfrew and S Shennan (eds) *Ranking, Resource and Exchange*, 79–88. Cambridge: Univ Press.

Haselgrove, C C 1984. The later pre-Roman Iron Age between the Humber and the Tyne, in P R Wilson, R F J Jones and D M Evans (eds), *Settlement and Society in the Roman North*, 9–25. Bradford.

Haselgrove, C C 1987. *Iron Age Coinage in South-East England: the archaeological context*. Oxford: BAR 174.

Haselgrove, C C 1989. The later Iron Age in southern Britain and beyond, in M Todd (ed), *Research on Roman Britain 1960–89*, 1–18. London: Britannia Monogr 11.

Haselgrove, C C 1997. Iron Age brooch deposition and chronology, in Gwilt and Haselgrove (eds) 1997, 51–72.

Haselgrove, C C 1999a. The Iron Age, in Hunter and Ralston (eds) 1999, 113–134.

Haselgrove, C C 1999b. Iron Age societies in central Britain: retrospect and prospect, in Bevan (ed) 1999, 253–278.

Haselgrove, C C and McCullagh, R 2000. *An Iron Age Coastal Community in East Lothian: the excavation of two later prehistoric enclosure complexes at Fisher's Road, Port Seton, 1994–95*. Edinburgh: Scott Trust for Archaeol Res Monogr 6.

Hayes, R H, Hemingway, J E and Spratt, D A 1980. The distribution and lithology of beehive querns in north-east Yorkshire, *J Archaeol Sci* 7, 297–324.

Hedges, R E M, Pettitt, P B, Bronk Ramsey, C, and Van Klinken, G J 1988. Radiocarbon dates from the Oxford AMS system, Archaeometry Datelist 25, *Archaeometry* 40, 236.

Henderson, J 1989a. The evidence for regional production of Iron Age glass in Britain, in M Feugère (ed), *Le Verre Préromain en Europe Occidentale*, 63–72. Montagnac: Editions Monique Mergoil.

Henderson, J 1989b. The scientific analysis of ancient glass and its archaeological interpretation, in J

Henderson (ed), *Scientific Analysis in Archaeology*, 30–62. Oxford: OUCA Monogr 19.

Heron, C, Evershed, R P, Goad, L J and Denham, V 1991. New approaches to the analyses of organic residues from archaeological ceramics, in P Budd, B Chapman, *et al.* (eds), *Archaeological Sciences 1989*, 332–339. Oxford: Oxbow Monogr 9.

Heslop, D H 1988. The study of beehive querns, *Scott Archaeol Rev* 5, 59–65

Hey, G, Bayliss, A and Boyle, A 1999. Iron Age inhumation burials at Yarnton, Oxfordshire, *Antiquity* 73, 551–562.

Hill, J D 1995a. *Ritual and Rubbish in the Iron Age of Wessex*. Oxford: BAR 242.

Hill, J D. 1995b. How should we study Iron Age societies and hillforts? A contextual study from Southern England, in Hill and Cumberpatch (eds) 1995, 45–66.

Hill, J D 1995c. The pre-Roman Iron Age in Britain and Ireland: an overview, *J World Prehist* 9(1), 47–98.

Hill, J D 1997. 'The end of one kind of body and the beginning of another kind of body?' Toilet instruments and 'Romanization' in southern England during the first century AD, in Gwilt and Haselgrove (eds) 1997, 96–107.

Hill, J D 1999. Settlement, landscape and regionality: Norfolk and Suffolk in the pre-Roman Iron Age of Britain and beyond, in J A Davies and T Williamson (eds), *Land of the Iceni: the Iron Age in northern East Anglia*, 185–207. Norwich: Stud E Anglian Hist 4.

Hill, J D forthcoming. Not just about the potter's wheel: Making, using and depositing pots in Middle and Late Iron Age East Anglia, in Woodward and Hill forthcoming.

Hill, J D and Cumberpatch, C G (eds), *Different Iron Ages: studies on the Iron Age in temperate Europe*. Oxford: BAR S602.

Hill, J D and Braddock, P forthcoming. The Iron Age pottery from Haddenham V, in Evans and Hodder forthcoming.

Hill, P H 1982. Broxmouth hill-fort excavations, 1977–8: an interim report, in Harding (ed) 1982, 141–88.

Hillam, J 1992. Dendrochronology in England; the dating of a wooden causeway from Lincolnshire and a log boat from Humberside, *Actes du XIIIe Colloque AFEAF, Guérat, 1989*, 137–141. Guérat.

Hingley, R 1990. Boundaries surrounding Iron Age and Romano-British settlements, *Scott Archaeol Rev* 7, 96–103.

Hingley, R 1992. Society in Scotland from 700 BC to AD 200, *Proc Soc Antiq Scot* 122, 7–53.

Hingley, R 1995. The Iron Age in Atlantic Scotland: searching for the meaning of the substantial house, in Hill and Cumberpatch (eds) 1995, 185–194.

Hingley, R. 1997. Iron, ironworking and regeneration: a study of the symbolic meaning of metalworking in Iron Age Britain, in Gwilt and Haselgrove (eds) 1997, 9–18.

Hingley, R 1999. The creation of later prehistoric landscapes and the context of the re-use of Neolithic and earlier Bronze Age monuments in Britain and Ireland, in Bevan (ed) 1999, 233–251.

Hobbs, R 1996. *British Iron Age Coins in the British Museum*. London: Brit Mus.

Hodder, I and Hedges, J W 1977. 'Weaving combs': their typology and distribution with some introductory remarks on date and function, in J R Collis (ed), *The Iron Age in Britain – a review*, 17–28. Sheffield: Dept Prehist Archaeol.

Hodder I R and Evans, C forthcoming. *The Haddenham Project*. E Anglian Archaeol.

Hughes, G 1994. Old Oswestry hillfort: excavations by W J Varley 1939–40, *Archaeol Cambrensis* 143, 46–91.

Hull, M R and Hawkes, C F C 1987. *Pre-Roman Bow Brooches*. Oxford: BAR 168.

Hunter, F 1997. Iron Age hoarding in Scotland and northern England, in Gwilt and Haselgrove (eds) 1997, 108–133.

Hunter, F 1998a. Cannel coal, in D H Caldwell, G Ewart and J Triscott, Auldhill, Portencross, *Archaeol J* 155, 42–53.

Hunter, F 1998b. Lead, in L Main, Excavation of a timber round-house and broch at the Fairy Knowe, Buchlyvie, Stirlingshire, 1975–8, *Proc Soc Antiq Scot* 128, 352–356.

Hunter, F forthcoming. The carnyx in Iron Age Europe, *Antiq J* 81 (2001).

Hunter, F, McDonnell, J G, Pollard, A M, Morris, C R and Rowlands, C C, 1993. The scientific identification of archaeological jet-like artefacts, *Archaeometry* 35, 69–89.

Hunter, J R and Ralston, I B M (eds) 1999. *The Archaeology of Britain. An Introduction from the Upper Palaeolithic to the Industrial Revolution*. London: Routledge.

Hutcheson, A R J 1997. Native or Roman? Ironwork hoards in northern Britain, in K Meadows, C Lemke and J Heron (eds), *TRAC 96: Proceedings of the 6th Annual Theoretical Roman Archaeology Conference*, 65–72. Oxford: Oxbow.

James, S 1999 *The Atlantic Celts: ancient people or modern invention?* London: Brit Mus.

James, S and Millett, M (eds) 2001. Briton and Roman: advancing an archaeological agenda. York: CBA Res Rep 125.

James, S and Rigby, V 1997. Britain and the Celtic Iron Age. London: British Museum.

Jersey, P de, Hooker, J, and Perron, C 2001. Celtic Coin Index on Line, http://units.ox.ac.uk/departments/archaeology/ccindex/ccindex.htm

Jobey, G 1974. Excavations at Boonies, Westerkirk, and the nature of Romano-British settlement in eastern Dumfriesshire, *Proc Soc Antiq Scot* 105, 119–140.

Jones, M K 1981. The development of crop husbandry, in Jones and Dimbleby (eds) 1981, 95–127.

Jones, M K 1984. The plant remains, in Cunliffe 1984, 483–495.

Jones, M K 1985. Archaeobotany beyond subsistence reconstruction, in Barker and Gamble (eds) 1985, 107–128.

Jones, M K 1996. Plant Exploitation, in Champion and Collis (eds) 1996, 29–40.

Jones, M K and Dimbleby, G W (eds) 1981. *The Environment of man: the Iron Age to Anglo-Saxon period*. Oxford: BAR 87.

Jope, E M 2000. *Early Celtic Art in the British Isles*. Oxford.

Kennett, D H 1977. Shale vessels of the late Pre-Roman Iron Age: context, distribution and origins, *Bedfordshire Archaeol J* 12, 17–22.

Kilbride-Jones, H E 1938. Glass armlets in Britain, *Proc Soc Antiq Scot* 72, 366–395.

Knight, D forthcoming. A regional ceramic sequence: pottery of the first millennium BC between the Humber and the Nene, in Woodward and Hill (eds) forthcoming.

Lane, A 1990. Hebridean pottery: problems of definition, chronology, presence and absence, in I Armit (ed), *Beyond the Brochs*, 108–130. Edinburgh: Univ Press.

Lawson, A J 2000. *Potterne 1982–5: animal husbandry in later prehistoric Wiltshire*. Salisbury: Wessex Archaeol Rep 17.

Lynn, C J 1977. Trial excavations at the King's Stables, Tray Townland, County Armagh, *Ulster J Archaeol* 40, 42–62.

Macdonald, P 2000. *A Reassessment of the Copper Alloy Artefacts from the Llyn Cerrig Bach, Anglesey, Assemblage*. Unpubl Ph D thesis, Univ Wales, Cardiff.

Macdonald, P forthcoming. *The Copper Alloy Artefacts from Llyn Cerrig Bach, Anglesey*. Univ of Wales Press.

MacGregor, M 1976. *Early Celtic Art in North Britain*. Leicester: Univ Press.

Mackie, E W 1982. The Leckie broch, Stirlingshire: an interim report, *Glasgow Archaeol J* 9, 60–72

Mackreth, D 1994. Late La Tène brooch, in R Thorpe and J Sharman, An Iron Age and Romano-British enclosure system at Normanton-le-Heath, Leicestershire, *Trans Leicestershire Archaeol Hist Soc* 68, 49–50.

Maltby, M 1981. Iron Age, Romano-British and Anglo-Saxon animal husbandry: a review of the faunal evidence, in Jones and Dimbleby (eds) 1981, 155–204.

Maltby, M 1985. Patterns in faunal assemblage variability, in Barker and Gamble (eds) 1985, 33–74.

Maltby, M 1996. The exploitation of animals in the Iron Age: the archaeo-zoological evidence, in Champion and Collis (eds) 1996, 17–27.

Manning, W and Saunders, C 1972. A socketed iron axe from Maid's Moreton, Buckinghamshire and a note on the type, *Antiq J* 52, 276–292.

Mays, M (ed) 1992. *Celtic Coinage: Britain and Beyond*. Oxford: BAR 222.

McDonnell, J G 1987. Ore to artefact – a study of early ironworking technology, in Slater and Tate (eds) 1987, 283–293.

McOmish, D 1996. East Chisenbury: ritual and rubbish in the British Bronze Age–Iron age transition, *Antiquity* 70, 68–76.

Morris, E L 1985. Prehistoric salt distributions: two case studies from western Britain, *Bull Board Celtic Stud* 32, 336–379.

Morris, E L 1994. Production and distribution of pottery and salt in Iron Age Britain: a review, *Proc Prehist Soc* 60, 371–393.

Morris, E L 1996. Iron Age artefact production and exchange, in Champion and Collis (eds) 1996, 41–65.

Morris, E L, Earl, G, Poppy, S, Westcott, K and Champion, T C 1998. *The Later Prehistoric Pottery Collections Register and Bibliography for England: a Gazetteer*. Report for English Heritage on behalf of the Prehistoric Ceramics Research Group, Univ Southampton.

Morris, E L, and Champion, T C 2001. Seven thousand collections – on the web, *Antiquity* 75, 253–4.

Munro, R 1882. *Ancient Scottish Lake-Dwellings or Crannogs*. Edinburgh: David Douglas.

Murphy, K 1992. Plas Gogerddan, Dyfed: a multi-period burial and ritual site, *Archaeol J* 149, 1–38.

Musson, C R, Britnell, W J, Northover, J P and Salter, C J 1992. Excavations and metal-working at Llwyn Bryn-dinas hillfort, Llangedwyn, Clwyd, *Proc Prehist Soc* 58, 265–283.

Nayling, N and Caseldine, A 1997. *Excavations at Caldicot, Gwent: Bronze Age palaeochannels in the Lower Nedern Valley*. York: CBA Res Rep 108.

Needham, S and Ambers, J 1994. Re-dating Rams Hill and reconsidering Bronze Age enclosure, *Proc Prehist Soc* 60, 225–243.

Needham, S P and Spence, T 1997. Refuse and the formation of middens, *Antiquity* 71, 77–90.

Needham, S, Bronk Ramsay, C, Coombs, D, Cartwright, C, and Pettitt, P 1998. An independent chronology for British Bronze Age metalwork: the results of the Oxford radiocarbon accelerator programme, *Archaeol J* 154, 55–107.

Neville, M (ed) 1999. *Living on the Edge of Empire: models, methodology and marginality*. Manchester: Archaeol North–West 3.

Niblett, R 1999. *The Excavation of a Ceremonial Site at Folly Lane, Verulamium.* London: Britannia Monogr 14.

Northover, J P 1987. Copper, tin, silver and gold in the Iron Age, in Slater and Tate (eds) 1987, 223–234.

Northover, J P 1992. Materials issues in the Celtic coinage, in Mays (eds) 1992, 235–299.

Northover, P 1984. Iron Age bronze metallurgy in Central Southern England, in Cunliffe and Miles (eds) 1984, 126–145.

Olivier, A. 1996. *Frameworks for Our Past.* London: English Heritage.

Oswald, A 1997. A doorway on the past: practical and mystic concerns in the orientation of roundhouse doorways, in Gwilt and Haselgrove (eds) 1997, 87–95.

Palk, N 1984. *Iron Age Bridle Bits from Britain.* Edinburgh: Univ Occas Pap 10.

Parfitt, K 1995. *Iron Age Burials from Mill Hill, Deal.* London: Brit Mus.

Parker Pearson, M 1996. Food, fertility and front doors in the first millennium BC, in Champion and Collis (eds) 1996, 117–132.

Parker Pearson, M 1999. Food, sex and death: cosmologies in the British Iron Age with particular reference to East Yorkshire, *Cambridge J Archaeol* 9, 43–69.

Parker Pearson, M and Sharples, N 1999. *Between Land and Sea: Excavations at Dun Vulan, South Uist.* Sheffield: Sheffield Academic Press.

PCRG 1995. *The Study of Later Prehistoric Pottery: general policies and guidelines for analysis and publication.* London: Prehistoric Ceramics Research Group Occas Pap 1–2.

Peacock, D P S 1987. Iron Age and Roman quern production at Lodsworth, West Sussex, *Antiq J* 67, 61–85.

Pearce, J 1997. Death and time: the structure of late Iron Age mortuary ritual, in Gwilt and Haselgrove (eds) 1997, 174–180.

Piggott, S 1950. Swords and scabbards of the British Early Iron Age, *Proc Prehist Soc* 16, 1–28.

Piggott, S 1966. A scheme for the Scottish Iron Age, in A L F Rivet (ed), *The Iron Age in Northern Britain,* 1–16. Edinburgh: Univ Press.

Prehistoric Society 1988. *Saving our Prehistoric Heritage.* London: Prehistoric Society.

Pryor, F 1996. Sheep, stocklands and farm systems: Bronze Age livestock populations in the Fenlands of eastern England, *Antiquity* 70, 313–324.

Raftery, B (ed) 1996. *Sites and Sights of the Iron Age.* Oxford: Oxbow Monogr 56.

RCAHMS 1994 *South-East Perth: an archaeological landscape.* London: HMSO.

Richards, J and Robinson, D (eds) 2001. *Digital Archives from Excavation and Fieldwork: guide to good practice* (2nd edn). York: Archaeol Data Service.

Rigby, V and Freestone, I 1997. Ceramic changes in Late Iron Age Britain, in I Freestone and D Gaimster (eds), *Pottery in the Making: World ceramic traditions,* 56–61. London: Brit Mus.

Robinson, M 1984. Landscape and environment of central southern Britain in the Iron Age, in Cunliffe and Miles (eds) 1984, 1–11.

Salter, C and Ehrenreich, R M 1984. Iron Age metallurgy in central southern Britain, in Cunliffe and Miles (eds) 1984, 146–161.

Saville, A and Hallén, Y 1994. The 'Obanian Iron Age': human remains from the Oban cave sites, Argyll, Scotland, *Antiquity* 68, 715–723.

Savory, H N 1976. *Guide Catalogue of the Early Iron Age Collections.* Cardiff: Nat Mus Wales.

Scott, B G 1991. *Early Irish Ironworking.* Belfast: Ulster Mus.

Sealey, P R 1997. The Iron Age in Essex, in O Bedwin (ed), *The Archaeology of Essex,* 46–68. Chelmsford: Essex County Council.

Sellwood, L 1984. Objects of bone and antler, in Cunliffe 1984, 371–395.

Sharples, N M 1990. Late Iron Age society and continental trade in Dorset, in A Duval, J-P Le Bihan and Y Menez (eds), *Les Gaulois d'Armorique: actes du XII colloque d'AFEAF, Quimper Mai 1988,* 299–304. Rennes: Revue Archéologique de l'Ouest Supplément 3.

Sharples, N M 1991a. Warfare in the Iron Age of Wessex, *Scott Archaeol Rev* 8, 79–89.

Sharples, N M 1991b. *Maiden Castle: excavation and field survey 1985–6.* London: English Heritage Archaeol Rep 19.

Sharples, N M 1998. *Scalloway: a broch, Late Iron Age settlement and medieval cemetery in Shetland.* Oxford: Oxbow Monogr 82.

Sharples, N M and Parker Pearson, M 1997. Why were brochs built? Recent studies in the Iron Age of Atlantic Scotland, in Gwilt and Haselgrove (eds) 1997, 254–65.

Sheridan, A, 1996. The Oldest Bow and other objects, *Current Archaeol* 149, 188–190.

Slater, E A and Tate, J O (eds) 1987. *Science and Archaeology,* Glasgow 1987. Oxford: BAR 196.

SPRS 1985. *Priorities for the Preservation and Excavation of Romano-British Sites.* London: Society for the Promotion of Roman Studies.

Stead, I M 1985. *The Battersea Shield.* London: Brit Mus.

Stead, I M 1991a. *Iron Age Cemeteries in East Yorkshire.* London: English Heritage.

Stead, I M 1991b. The Snettisham treasure: excavations in 1990, *Antiquity* 65, 447–465.

Stead, I M 1995. The metalwork, in K Parfitt 1995, 59–111.

Stead, I M 1998. *The Salisbury Hoard.* Stroud: Tempus.

40

Stevenson, R B K 1956. Native bangles and Roman glass, *Proc Soc Antiq Scot* 88, 208–221.

Stevenson, R B K 1976. Romano-British glass bangles, *Glasgow Archaeol J* 4, 45–54.

Stoertz, C 1997. *Ancient Landscapes of the Yorkshire Wolds.* London: RCHME.

Sunter, N and Woodward, P J 1987. *Romano-British Industries in Purbeck.* Dorchester: Dorset Natur Hist Archaeol Soc Monogr 6.

Swain, H P 1987. The Iron Age pottery, in D H Heslop, *The Excavation of an Iron Age Settlement at Thorpe Thewles, Cleveland, 1980–1982,* 57–71. London: CBA Res Rep 65.

Taylor, J 1997. Space and place: some thoughts on Iron Age and Romano-British landscapes, in Gwilt and Haselgrove (eds) 1997, 192–204.

Taylor, R J 1993. *Hoards of the Bronze Age in Southern Britain.* Oxford: BAR 228.

Taylor, R J and Brailsford, J W 1985. British Iron Age strap unions, *Proc Prehist Soc* 51, 247–272.

Thomas, N forthcoming. *Conderton Camp. Hereford and Worcester: a small middle Iron Age hillfort on Bredon Hill.* York: CBA Res Rep.

Tipping, R 1997. Pollen analysis and the impact of Rome on native agriculture around Hadrian's Wall, in Gwilt and Haselgrove (eds) 1997, 239–247.

Topping, P G 1987. Typology and chronology in the later prehistoric pottery assemblages of the Western Isles, *Proc Soc Antiq Scot* 117, 67–84.

Veen, M van der 1992. *Crop Husbandry Regimes: an archaeobotanical study of farming in northern England 1000 BC–AD 500.* Sheffield: Sheffield Archaeol Monogr 3.

Veen, M van der and O'Connor, T 1998. The expansion of agriculture in late Iron Age and Roman Britain, in Bayley (ed) 1998, 127–143.

Venclova, N 1991. Habitats industriels celtiques du IIIe siècle av. J.-C. en Bohême, *Etudes Celtiques* 28, 435–450.

Warner, R B 1993. Irish prehistoric Goldwork: a provisional analysis, *Archeomaterials* 7, 101–113.

Warrilow, W, Owen, G and Britnell, W 1986. Eight ring-ditches at Four Crosses, Llandysilio, Powys 1981–85, *Proc Prehist Soc* 52, 53–87.

Watkins, T 1980. Excavation of an Iron Age open settlement at Dalladies, Kincardineshire, *Proc Soc Antiq Scot* 110, 122–164.

Whimster, R 1989. *The Emerging Past: air photography and the buried landscape.* London: English Heritage.

Whittle, A W R 1989. Two later Bronze Age occupations and an Iron Age channel on the Gwent foreshore, *Bull Board Celtic Stud* 36, 200–223.

Williamson, T 1987. Early co-axial field systems on the East Anglian boulder clays, *Proc Prehist Soc* 53, 419–431.

Williams, G 1985. *An Iron Age Cremation Deposit from Castle Bucket Letterston, Pembrokeshire,* Archaeol Wales 25, 13–15.

Willis, S H 1994. Roman imports into Late Iron Age: British societies: Towards a critique of existing models, in S Cottam, D Dungworth, S Scott and J Taylor (eds), *TRAC 94: Proc 4th Theoretical Roman Archaeology Conference, Durham 1994,* 141–150. Oxford.

Willis, S H, 1995. The briquetage, in P Abramson, A Late Iron Age settlement at Scotch Corner, North Yorkshire, *Durham Archaeol J* 11, 7–18.

Willis, S H 1996. The Romanization of pottery assemblages in the East and North-East of England during the first century AD: a comparative analysis, *Britannia* 27, 179–221.

Willis, S H 1997. Settlement, materiality and landscape in the Iron Age of the East Midlands. evidence, interpretation and wider resonance, in Gwilt and Haselgrove (eds) 1997, 205–15.

Willis, S H 1999. Without and within: aspects of culture and community in the Iron Age of north-east England, in Bevan (eds) 1999, 81–110.

Willis, S H forthcoming. *An Archaeological Resource Assessment of the later Bronze Age and Iron Age in the East Midland Counties of England.* Leicester.

Wilson, B 1978. The animal bones, in M Parrington (ed), *The Excavation of an Iron Age Settlement, Bronze Age Ring Ditches and Roman Features at Ashville Trading Estate, Abingdon (Oxfordshire) 1974–6,* 110–139. London: CBA Res Rep 28.

Wilson, D 1983. Pollen analysis and settlement archaeology of the first millennium bc from north-east England, in J C Chapman and H C Mytum (eds), *Settlement in North Britain 1000 BC–AD 1000,* 29–54. Oxford: BAR 118.

Woodward, A B 1997. Size and style: an alternative study of some Iron Age pottery in southern England, in Gwilt and Haselgrove (eds) 1997, 26–35.

Woodward, A and Blinkhorn, P W 1997. Size is important: Iron Age vessel capacities in central and southern England, in C G Cumberpatch and P W Blinkhorn (eds), *Not so Much a Pot, More a Way of Life,* 153–162. Oxford: Oxbow Monogr 83.

Woodward, A and Hill, J D (eds) forthcoming. *Prehistoric Britain: the ceramic basis.* Oxford: Oxbow Mongr.

Yates, D T 1999. Bronze Age field systems in the Thames Valley, *Oxford J Archaeol* 18, 157–70.

Young, R and Humphrey, J 1999. Flint use in England after the Bronze Age: time for a re-evaluation? *Proc Prehist Soc* 65, 231–242.

Index

Figures in bold indicate illustrations

hillforts 5, 6, 8, 14, 27, 29
Historic Scotland 1, 5
Holme-next-the-Sea, Norfolk 6
Howe, Orkney 7
human remains (*see* burials *and* dating)

iron 2, 19
 ironworking 18, 22, 29, 31

Kemerton, Herefordshire 11
King Harry Lane, St Albans, Hertfordshire 3
Kirkchrist, Wigtownshire, wooden bowl from **6**
Kimmeridge shale 18, 20

landscapes 10–12, 27–8, 31
La Tène 3, **16**, 17, 24
lead/leadworking 21
Little Woodbury, Wiltshire 9
Llyn Carrig Bach, Anglesey, metalwork deposit 6, 17
Llyn Fawr hoard 27

Maiden Castle, Dorset 9, 11, 29, 30
material culture studies 2, 3, 14–22, 23, Table 4
Merthyr Mawr, Glamorgan 9
metal-detecting **15**, 16, 22, 26
metalwork 3, 6, 16, Table 2, 21–2, 24, 26, **26**, 30, 31
 bronze shield **16**
 brooches 3, 17
 deposits 6, 11, 19, 21, 25–7, 31
 harness 11, 17, 18
 jewellery **15**, 21
 Late Bronze Age 6
 socketed axes **26**, 27
 swords 17
 torcs 11, **15**, 21, 30
 (*see also* coins, lead, precious metals)
metalworking 11, 21, 26–7, 31
 objects associated with 21, 27 (*see also* ironworking)
midden sites 27
Moel-y-Gaer, Flintshire 9
Mucking, Essex 9

Newbridge, Midlothian, chariot burial **13**
Nettleton Copse, Wherwell, Hampshire 7

oppida 29, 30, **30**
organic finds **6**, 19–20, **20**, Table 1

Penllyn Moor, S. Glamorgan, socketed axe from **26**
Portable Antiquities 16, 22
pottery 3, 4, 16, 17, Table 2, 21, **21**, 26, 28, 29, 30
 dating of 6, 30, 31
 organic residues on 5, 19

PPG 16 1, 7, 9
precious metals 21, 30
publication Table 4

regionality 2, 22–5, Table 3
regional research strategies/frameworks 1, 24–5
ritual 8, 9, 10, Table 4
 behaviour 8, 14, 23, 26, 30
 'rubbish' 8, 10
 sites 7, 8, 19, **19** 29, 30 (*see also* votive deposits)
Rudston, E. Yorkshire 7

salt/saltworking 11, 18, 27
 briquetage 21
sampling *see* environmental evidence
settlements/settlement patterns 2, 7–14, 26, 27–8, 29, 31, Table 4
 boundaries 10, 14, 27
 farmsteads/field systems 10, 29
 'open' 9, 10, 14, **28**
 pit alignments **27**
 enclosures **23, 29**
 wells/pits 27
shrines *see* ritual sites
Silchester, Hampshire 30, **30**
Somerset lake villages 6
 Glastonbury 15
Severn Estuary 2, **2**, 26, 29
Snettisham, Norfolk, hoard 21
St Albans, Hertfordshire 30 (*see also* King Harry Lane)
St Catherine's Hill, Hampshire 11
Stanwick, N. Yorkshire **30**
stone objects 20–1, Table 2
Suddern Farm, Middle Wallop, Hampshire **8**

textiles/skins 20, Table 1
Thorpe Thewles, Cleveland 7
Traprain Law, East Lothian 9, 11, **11**
transition
 late Bronze Age–earlier Iron Age 25–6, 31
 earlier Iron Age–later pre-Roman Iron Age 28–9, 31
 middle–late Iron Age 29

Westhampnett, W. Sussex 7, 12, 30
West Harling, Norfolk 9
Wetwang Slack, E. Yorkshire 14, **14**
wetland/waterlogged sites 6, 15, 29
Winchester Hoard **15**
wooden objects **6**, 20, Table 1
woodland 10

votive deposits 16, 18–19, 27

Yarnton, Oxfordshire **4**, 5